As They Appear

Books by JOHN MASON BROWN

JOHN MASON BROWN

As They Appear

HAMISH HAMILTON
London

First published in Britain, 1953, by HAMISH HAMILTON LTD.

814

BRO

214492:

Printed in the United States of America

Thanks are due, and once more gladly given, to *The Saturday Review* for permission to reprint these selections from SEEING THINGS, a department appearing almost weekly in its pages

Contents

Contents

· viii ·

Men and Books

THE CONFESSIONS of a man who knows more about Horace Walpole than even Horace Walpole knew, and the gulf which separates the reader, however constant, from the true collector.

᷾᷾᷾᷾᷾᷾᷾᷾᷾᷾᷾᷾᷾᷾᷾᷾᷾᷾᷾᷾᷾᷾᷾᷾᷾᷾᷾᷾᷾᷾᷾᷾

Ex Libris

A STORY has it that, though General Eisenhower liked Kenneth S. Davis's biography of him when he finally got around to reading it, he did not read it at once. Davis had spent months with the General while working on *Soldier of Democracy*. Naturally, when it was rushed off the presses in 1945, he was anxious to have Eisenhower's opinion of it.

"Thanks a lot for the book, Kenneth," the General is reported to have said when given a copy, "but I don't promise to read it." Then, an overworked and modest man, he added, smiling, "After all, you've lived with me for only one year and I've had to live with me for fifty-five years. So I can't see how you could possibly tell me anything about myself that I don't already know."

Horace Walpole devoted nearly eighty years, and Wilmarth Lewis has so far devoted only twenty-seven, to living with Horace Walpole. Yet it seems safe to say that Mr. Lewis knows more about Walpole; the books he wrote, printed, owned, or read; his possessions at Strawberry Hill, and his correspondence than Walpole did himself, and he knew a great deal. Walpole while living his life must, as mortals will, have forgotten some of its details. Mr. Lewis, in reliving it for him, has forgotten nothing.

More than being Mr. Lewis's hobby, Walpole is his lifework. Everything and everyone connected with Walpole is of passionate concern to him. Active though he is on many boards, Mr. Lewis could be a gentleman of leisure if only Walpole's shade were gentlemanly enough to leave him alone. But, fortunately for scholarship and all students of the eighteenth century, it will not.

Mr. Lewis's devotion to Walpole is boundless and knows no fatigue. After all, he is editing the monumental *Yale Edition of Horace Walpole's Correspondence,* of which fourteen volumes have already appeared. Sixteen more are now well along, and the final one (the fiftieth?) he hopes to publish in 1965 on his seventieth birthday. Mr. Lewis's preoccupation with Walpole does not stop there. He has turned Twickenham's first citizen into a resident of Connecticut. In his charming colonial house at Farmington Mr. Lewis has brought together thousands upon thousands of the long-scattered books, letters, paintings, manuscripts, and relics which were once to be found at Strawberry Hill. If wisely he has not attempted to reproduce the Gothic oddities of that toy castle of Walpole's creation, he has succeeded in assembling the world's greatest collection of Walpoliana.

Collector's Progress * is Mr. Lewis's account of how his fabulous collection came into being. It is an engaging book for many reasons. Its tone is warm and personal; its touch light and relaxed. Its wit is as lively as that which makes Mr. Lewis one of the most captivating of conversationalists and speakers. It

* *Collector's Progress,* by Wilmarth Lewis. New York: Alfred A. Knopf. 253 pp. $5.

is a record of triumphs recounted without boasting and some failures honestly and humorously described; a yarn of pursuit and detection which happens to be true. It is also a chronicle of friendships, with enchanting tributes paid to the booksellers who have helped him and to such notable collectors who have guided him as the late Dr. Edward Clark Streeter and Yale's Chauncey Tinker. It is, too, a tale of adventure, a *Kon-Tiki* of the secondhand book stores and the auction rooms. Indeed, no book concerned with the quest of other books has equaled it in charm since A. Edward Newton's *The Amenities of Book Collecting*.

Most of us are collectors of one thing or another. We are fated to collect years if nothing else. Collecting on Mr. Lewis's scale, with his dedication and intensity and such a rigid sense of specialization, is a different matter. One is bound to wonder why such absorption in one man; why that particular man; why so much time, energy, and money selflessly given; and why the endless ramifications to which interest of this kind leads when it has swollen into zeal.

Francis Henry Taylor in *The Taste of Angels*, his brilliant history of art collections from the Egyptians down to Napoleon, speaks of the "sort of devil" which possesses collectors. That this is a very real and driving devil, no one can deny. Certainly Mr. Lewis would not. Yet, when it comes to books and the rarefied realm of first editions and pristine or mint copies, that devil has operated in ways beyond my comprehension. At least it has in the past. If it does not in the future, the reason is that Mr. Lewis has come nearer than anyone else to making me understand the importance—even the sanity—of bibliomania.

I collect more books than my budget can afford or my apartment can decently hold. Even so I am a poor collector in Mr. Lewis's sense, not only because I am poor but also because valuable books are utterly valueless to me. Since I cannot use them, I do not want them. And since I do not want them, I do not deserve them. Renegade that I am, I am not sufficiently craven to mutilate the few choice volumes I own. This much sense and this much reverence I have.

Nonetheless, so far as books are concerned, let me confess the hideous truth, I am a rapist. I want to possess them without asking their consent. There is a frigidity about museum items which I cannot abide. The books I love are not untouchables. I have no shelf or floor space for such volumes as would be violated if their leaves were cut. I cannot persuade myself that a book is worth owning, the sole merit of which is that it is rare. Cheap editions, if the type is good, are as dear to me as the most expensive. A book's value does not fluctuate, to my way of thinking, because the margins of its pages have been lessened by a millimeter. I am far fonder of original works than of original bindings.

As a writer, I hold uncut pages to be a comment on an owner and an insult to an author. A book for me is something to be read, not kept under glass or in a safe. I want to dog-ear it, to underline it, to annotate it, and mark favorite passages, and make my own index on the blank pages at the back. I prize the contents, not the exterior, the stuffs of literature rather than the printed object, however jewel-like. My desire is for a book to be a friend instead of a royal visitor, and to treat it with the kind of disrespect only affection makes possible. In short, in my own working library (which I love) I am by all the standards of a bibliographer the most contemptible of pariahs.

Mr. Lewis has opened my eyes wider than they have ever

been opened to that other world, the world of the real collectors. He has done this, first of all, by quoting some words spoken to him long ago by Chauncey Tinker. Professor Tinker, according to Mr. Lewis, was almost alone among university people in understanding the importance of possessing the first editions of the books he studied and taught.

Colleagues who said "The last edition is the best" with an air of having said something profound were consigned by him to the pit without argument. "How can you fully understand the effect of a book on its time unless you know what it looked like?" he would ask everyone but the Philistines, and with them he would not bother. Professor Tinker's contention was that collecting is a form of scholarship—exacting, imaginative, creative. Where, he would argue, would scholars be if there had been no collectors before them to bring together the books that make research possible? Collecting, libraries, publication, these three, he insisted, were vital, and the first of these—without which the other two would not exist—is collecting.

Mr. Lewis was obviously a born collector. And a born collector is as uncommon as a born singer, a born writer, painter, architect, warrior, or statesman. He came to be, not *a* Walpole man, but *the* Walpole man by a process of evolution crossed with chance. He began by hoarding houseflies in a discarded cigar box when he was five. The following year he switched to shells. Inevitably the next move was to stamps. From having been a devoted philatelist, he turned into a no less devoted numismatist. From coins he changed to butterflies. It was not until he was a Yale freshman that he became a book collector, an interest he temporarily misplaced when he bought a copy of *Alice in Wonderland* under the impression it was a first edition until someone pointed out that its title-page bore a New York imprint and the line "Seventy-seventh thousand."

After the First World War Mr. Lewis returned to Yale, and when John Masefield lectured there he applied himself to collecting Masefield's works. Subsequent trips abroad found him haunting old book shops and bagging his first treasures. Without realizing it, he was edging toward that fateful day when he would have to choose between being a general and a specialized collector.

His purchase in England of some manuscript notes by Lady Louisa Stuart attached in a pocket to the front cover of the first volume of John Heneage Jesse's *George Selwyn and His Contemporaries* led him to do some research during which he encountered Walpole's name again and again. Before he knew it, and due to his picking up for a song at Scribner's some valuable Strawberry Hill Press publications, including Gray's *Odes*, Mr. Lewis had made his decision. He had turned down the "narrow, weed-grown road" that led to Horace Walpole, that road which he was to clear of its weeds and turn into a main highway.

Mr. Lewis has long been well aware that few writers have fluctuated more in critical esteem than Walpole. To Lord David Cecil, Walpole was "more like a sprite than a man" with "his dragonfly elegance." Virginia Woolf thought him "the strangest mixture of ape and cupid that ever was." Macaulay described him as "a pâté-de-foie-gras . . . made of livers preternaturally swollen." To Croker he was a poisoner of history at its source. Carlyle saw him as "a small, steady light . . . unusually accurate . . . an irrefragible authority." Byron was convinced that he was "surely worthy of a higher place than any living writer, be he who he may."

If, when he began to concentrate on Walpole, Mr. Lewis had any doubts, Professor Tinker helped to remove them. He exonerated Walpole of the charge of being responsible by his lordly indifference for Chatterton's death. He made clear the ignored importance of a dilettante and a gossip held to be trivial. Accordingly Mr. Lewis went ahead, and as he did so he came increasingly to see that exceptional as Walpole was as a personality, a writer, a correspondent, and a collector, he was more than that. He was the epitome of eighteenth-century England.

Over the years Mr. Lewis's collection has grown beyond his most ambitious dreams when he started it. From the books printed and written by Walpole, it has branched out to include every edition of his works; as many as possible of the books he owned; books written by his friends or dealing with subjects which interested him; volumes in which Walpole or his circle were mentioned; every obtainable Walpole manuscript, and the originals of the letters he sent and received; such relics as could be found that had once been in Strawberry Hill; and finally (at least for an overbold interval) the acquisition of every book published in England between 1751 and 1800 which was not already in the Yale Library.

In amassing the roomfuls of Walpoliana at Farmington Mr. Lewis has had his moments of high good fortune. To use a word of Walpole's which has come again into circulation, he has had the advantage of serendipity, "that faculty of making happy and accidental discoveries while looking for one thing and finding another." Mr. Lewis's persistence, however, has been greater than his luck. It has been equaled only by his endowments as a detective, his Geiger-counter instinct, his scholarship, his genius for friendship, and his unflagging fervor.

Macaulay's claim was that "scarcely any writer has ever troubled himself so much about the appearance which his works were to make before posterity" as Horace Walpole did. Surely few writers have ever been so fortunate as he has been in finding in Mr. Lewis a collector to assure his place in history. The new, the colonial Strawberry Hill at Farmington will in time be given, with all its treasures, to Yale. "To make a collection that stores up something of importance to society and then place it at society's disposal is to store up civilization for posterity's use," says Mr. Lewis. This is precisely what he has done. He has performed heroically an heroic work for scholarship and written about it with infinite modesty, charm, and urbanity in *Collector's Progress.*

September 22, 1951

OSCAR WILDE'S wisdom in persuading Ada Leverson, a lady as witty as she was wise, to bring the sparkle of her conversation to novel-writing.

Edwardian Sphinx

A FEW DAYS before Ada Leverson died in London in August 1936, a man, an old friend, dropped by to ask how she was. Her condition was serious but not too serious for her to insist upon making up her face before he was allowed to see her. When her daughter showed him in she was guilty of one of those sickroom lies all of us tell out of kindness. "Isn't Mother wonderful!" she exclaimed. "She'll soon be the same as everyone else." With effort Ada Leverson managed to sit bolt upright in bed. "That, thank God," she said, enunciating very clearly, "is one thing I shall never be!" Nor was she.

It is Sir Osbert Sitwell who tells this engaging story about her, along with many another, in *Noble Essences*. But it is Ada Leverson herself who demonstrates her singularity on almost every page of *The Limit*,* that novel of hers, one of the six she wrote between 1907 and 1916, which has just been published in America for the first time some forty years after it appeared in England.

I must admit the name Ada Leverson meant nothing to me until by his *Noble Essences* Sir Osbert had teased me into want-

* *The Limit*, by Ada Leverson. New York: W. W. Norton & Co. 256 pp. $3.

ing to know more—much more—about her. I should have been familiar with her works and reputation. On many counts she deserves remembrance as one of those figures who, though minor, are minor in a major way. I had read about her in many books on Wilde, especially in Hesketh Pearson's *Oscar Wilde: His Life and Wit.* Even so, her name had not stuck. It had floated into my consciousness and out again, as references will to those who, because we bring no associations to them, give our memories the slip. From now on, however, thanks to Sir Osbert, to W. W. Norton her American publisher, to a rereading of Hesketh Pearson, and a delighted gobbling up of *The Limit,* I do not think I shall ever forget Ada Leverson.

She comes down to us, shadowy but inviting, possessed of a warmth which death has not chilled. She survives her dying the way she outlasted Edwardian England and *Yellow Book* literature, a worldly yet enigmatic personality swathed in a sense of mystery as enfolding as the copious black cloak which in her last years she was fond of wearing by day. We think we know her. Then we realize that we do not, at least not quite, in spite of all the testimony and the tributes of those fortunate enough to have done so.

I may be wrong but I have been persuaded to see her, young or old, at the apex of her career or in the autumn of her recollections, as a woman having very much the appearance and intensity of Bernhardt but with a mellowness Sarah could not claim. She seems always to be not so much talking as purring, saying things wise, witty, or captivating in their absurdity, and saying them so low that one must strain to catch them, particularly when in her final years she had grown deaf (a sorry fate for a wit) and chose to mask her handicap by avoiding those shrill empty tones which are the give-away of the hard of hearing.

Oscar Wilde christened Ada Leverson "the Sphinx." No doubt he did this because, pale of face, red of lips, and slightly Aubrey Beardsley as she had been in the days of their friendship, she must have had that "minion of the moon" look which Oscar insisted in a note to her was the requisite of sphinxes. Apparently she never lost that look. Even in the last sixteen years of her life, when Sir Osbert came to know her well and she seemed an old lady, it was still to the Sphinx that, according to him, she bore a certain resemblance in the shape of her head and the molding of her features.

She was, however, a smiling Sphinx, blessed with the wisdom of laughter. Though she had suffered her full burden of sorrows—the loss of her only son as a small boy, the death of most of her literary contemporaries, the shrinkage of her fortune, the disgrace and pillorying of such a friend as Wilde, the coming of deafness, and the passing of the society into which she had been born—her blue eyes retained their gaiety to the end. Her friends would find her, Sir Osbert says, in the vast public room of the London hotel at which she stayed, "a little figure in black, sitting on a large sofa, a black satin bag and a paper-bound French book by her side, quite alone, but shaking with quiet irrepressible laughter." "Though the lines of her face were serious," he points out elsewhere, "her general and natural expression was a smile, not caused by any wish to mock, but by some absurdity she had detected in the world at large."

As a conversationalist Ada Leverson must have been enchanting. Sir Osbert gives many examples of her readiness with a phrase, the sudden mischief of her mind, and its originality.

Tempting as these are, none, I think, excels or could be more suggestive of her talk at its best than her comment when she heard that Sir Osbert's fabulously eccentric father had moved from the London hotel at which he usually stayed into Batt's Hotel in Albemarle Street. In her airiest manner she said, "I see your father's changed belfries."

Ada Leverson's courage was as great as her wit. She was one of the few of Wilde's friends who stood by him through his trials, during his imprisonment, and after his release. It was she and her husband, Ernest, who gave him refuge in their house between the two trials though not until after Mr. Leverson had called the servants together, telling them who was coming and offering them a month's wages if they wished to leave, which none of them did.

Although her first novel did not appear until seven years after his death, Oscar Wilde is no less inescapably linked with Ada Leverson as a writer than as a person. He had known her in the days when she was contributing sketches and parodies to *Punch, Black-and-White,* and the *Yellow Book,* and had valued her qualities at once, doubtless because he recognized in hers a touch in many ways like his own. "You have all the equipment of a writer, my dear Sphinx," he had said, "except pen, ink, and paper."

Fortunately, as *The Limit* proves, Ada Leverson forced herself in time to come by these material essentials. Her novel is a joy—light, slight, and mannered, but with wisdom shining through its absurdities and delectable because of the polish and distinction of its artifice. If it speaks engagingly for Mrs. Leverson, giving us shimmering indications of what her prowess must have been in conversation, it speaks no less wittily for Wilde. English critics, I notice, have endeavored to capture the merits and texture of *The Limit* by likening it to the work of a more amiable Saki, a less fantastic Ronald Firbank, or a more substantial Hope of *The Dolly Dialogues*. Yet in their search for a fit comparison it seems to me they have, in the best tradition of *The Vision of Sir Launfal*, traveled far and overlooked a figure who was right at their doorsteps and in her heyday at Ada Leverson's. I mean Oscar himself.

For *The Limit* reads the way a Wilde comedy ought to be played. Not a revival of one of his earlier dramas such as *Lady Windermere's Fan, A Woman of No Importance,* or *An Ideal Husband,* tarnished as their brilliance was by plots borrowed from French problem plays. No. A revival of a comedy by the Wilde who had escaped from Dumas-fils, Augier, and Sardou, and who in *The Importance of Being Earnest* had come wholly and jubilantly into his nonsensical own. Moreover, *The Limit* is a revival uncursed by any indifferent actors who cannot master the artificiality of the style, the ping-pong of the epigrams, or the deliciousness of the fooling. It would be ridiculous to say that it has Wilde's final polish, his ultimate arrogance of mind, grace of paradox, elegance of mockery, or brilliance. Even so, the spirit is often the same. And so is the tone.

The Limit tells how an English woman, who tries to marry off her younger sister to a rich American, is finally won back by her stupid husband after having had an affair. But its story is almost an irrelevance, its manner everything. Take Harry, the painter, for instance. "He had been educated for diplomacy, and learned eight languages, some of which he spoke fluently, and in all he could look with expression." Or Mr. Rathbone, who was so tattooed that his body was "really a kind of serial story—with illustrations" and the wonder was that "Lord Northcliffe doesn't bring him out in monthly parts." Or Romer whose wife, Valentia, "thought he looked very well through a window, and ought by rights always to be seen in that way—as it were, under glass." Or sharp-tongued old Mrs. Wyburn, Romer's mother, whose Wednesdays people enjoyed going to in order "to hear the nasty things she said about their friends."

Or Van Buren, the American millionaire, who "had a childish horror of vulgarity, and an innocent belief that an Englishman who had been to Eton and Oxford and who was *dans le mouvement*, smart and good-looking, and had deserted diplomacy for art, must of necessity be refined, superior, cultured, everything that Van Buren wanted to be." Or Vaughan, the fashionable playwright, who "was not even embittered by success." Or Miss Luscombe, the woman that those in the theatre thought was in society and those in society believed was on the stage. She "always wore an evening dress except in the evening." Once she came to a dinner party "dressed as if for Ascot" except for a great many strange ornaments to which "she added a cold."

The world into which *The Limit* leads us is a vanished universe. This is a part of the novel's fun and charm. It is a world within a world, confident of itself, minuscule in its interests, and trivial in its hopes. Love and profitable courtship are the chief worries of its characters. To these, as to marriage, they bring submerged, if any, emotions. When its men and women do not live by their wits, they live for them. No one, including themselves, could take them seriously. They do not have to tell jokes; they are jokes. They are sophisticates, protected, pampered, and spoiled, whose sole fear—a groundless one in their case—is the dread of being commonplace.

Readers who thrive on anguish, who like their reading purposeful, and who want all novels to be centered in the silo, the soil, or the soul, will find little to please and much to annoy them in *The Limit*. Most decidedly it is not their dish of tea. Instead, it is meant for those who find laughter no hardship, high comedy a delight, nonsense relaxing, and who are not made uncomfortable by worldlings both comfortable and conscienceless.

If, in spite of the good time I have had reading *The Limit*, I feel no particular urge to rush out and devour Ada Leverson's other five novels at one sitting, it is because a little of this kind of writing can go a long way. Nonetheless I am delighted to have made Ada Leverson's acquaintance and not to have missed *The Limit*.

Her novel is the kind of comedy at which the English excel. At least it is the kind of comedy at which they have excelled. It is the production of a top-drawer people at their top-drawer moment of international domination and personal security. It springs from the worldly prosperity, snobbishness, and class-consciousness in which high comedy flowers. Three hundred years of a Britannia that ruled the waves lie behind its assumptions, hence its values and laughter. Britons such as Evelyn Waugh and Nancy Mitford may write in a changed and threatened world wittily and brilliantly about the passage of an old and once entrenched society. One wonders, however, what will happen to the artifices of high comedy when that society has disappeared and the wealth is gone which enabled it to be not only idle but frivolous.

September 1, 1951

THE TWO Sir James Barries, the eter-
nal boy who was charming, and the prob-
lem child who became the victim of a
regrettable sprite called M'Connachie.

ᨠ·ᨠ

Sweetness and Blight

ALTHOUGH print seems permanent enough, it in no way guarantees permanence to a literary reputation. Most outstanding authors die at least twice; first, when death overtakes their bodies; next, when it overtakes their popularity. They may, of course, have lost their prestige long before their deaths. If they have not, they are apt to soon after their obituary praises have been sung. If they are blessed with the lasting as opposed to the evanescent stuffs, and if in the pendulum's swing there is a return to tastes and needs similar to those which once they satisfied, writers may be rediscovered and hence live again. When they survive a sufficient number of rediscoveries—more accurately, when they outlast the need to be rediscovered—they can be said to have taken their place among the immortals. In general, however, the disesteem into which they sink soon after dying is equal to the esteem in which they were held while alive.

The fate of Sir James Barrie is only the common lot. In spite of the current success of *Peter Pan* with Jean Arthur, the little man from Kirriemuir has gone into an eclipse. A revolt against him has taken place. How emphatic this reaction has been, Brooks Atkinson has made clear. Recently in the Sunday *New*

York Times, though praising *Peter Pan,* he said things about Barrie which thirty years ago would have caused the Messrs. Alexander Woollcott, Clayton Hamilton, and William Lyon Phelps to picket Mr. Ochs's journal and provoked mass demonstrations on the campuses of such female academies as Radcliffe, Bryn Mawr, and Vassar.

"Since Barrie was the man who would not grow up," wrote Mr. Atkinson, "most of his plays have no further significance in the theatre. . . . The world has dropped most of Barrie into the polite limbo of forgotten pleasures. Although he was a neat writer—neater than Shaw—his arch mannerisms and his demure mind do not have much value now. Aside from *The Admirable Crichton,* which almost makes a definite statement, there is very little of Barrie worth saving."

So sweeping a dismissal was bound to take some of us aback. We, too, would exempt *Peter Pan.* But, quite aside from feeling that *The Admirable Crichton* does make a definite statement, we would have our other entries of works by Barrie which we believe could be encountered even now with pleasure. *What Every Woman Knows* (especially because of its fine first act) is one of these. So is *Dear Brutus.* So is *Shall We Join the Ladies?* And *Mary Rose* and *The Boy David* are not without their champions, though I am not among them.

Forgetting the theatre, there are those of us who, whether we retain or have lost our first taste for *The Little Minister, Margaret Ogilvy,* or *A Window in Thrums,* continue to admire passages in *Courage,* that Rectorial Address which Barrie delivered in 1922 at St. Andrews. We still find amusement in his *Letters.* We wish we had heard those fugitive speeches of his collected under the title of *M'Connachie and J.M.B.* We are gratefully aware that Barrie was possessed of gifts, radiant and unique, which set him apart.

We also cannot bring ourselves to deny that famous, if dangerous, charm of his, nauseated as we may be by the excesses into which it so often misled him. Even so, it is impossible not to see Mr. Atkinson's point. A man who refused to grow up is fated to have less and less to say to a world desperately in need of growing up, in spite of the sorry daily reminders of its having failed to do so.

When *Peter Pan* was first produced in London Max Beerbohm noted that Barrie, earlier than most men who never come to maturity, had halted before the age when soldiers and steam engines begin to dominate the soul. "To remain, like Mr. Kipling, a boy, is not at all uncommon," said Beerbohm. "But I know not anyone who remains, like Mr. Barrie, a child." Beerbohm saluted *Peter Pan* as Barrie's best work because, as he stated it paradoxically, "Here at last we see his talent in its full maturity for here he has stripped off from himself the last flimsy remnants of a pretense of maturity."

The child's point of view, caught with ease and stated so that children recognize its truth, is what makes *Peter Pan* timeless. We are fools, therefore, if we, as elders, take the elderly with us to see the play. For complete enjoyment it is wisest to have in the seat next to you a young person of the proper credulity, perched on your folded overcoat and his, clutching at your hand, listening and looking with wide-eyed wonder at everything that is being said or done, and squealing with delight. What you and I think is, for the moment, beside the point. What a pint-sized companion thinks is all-important.

The intermissions are the true measure of the thralldom in which *Peter Pan* still holds those who have not grown up. Then it is that the aisles are turned into such runways as the busiest airports do not know. Little boys and girls, joyously freed from the blighting influence of their parents, can hardly wait to affirm their belief in Barrie's play. They jostle one another as, with their arms spread wide, they race up and down, prepared for that take-off which not only Peter but the Darling children have convinced them is within each small mortal's reach. The law of gravity being as obstinate as everything else that is prosaic on this planet, these juveniles remain carpet-bound. This, however, is an irrelevance. By rushing forward, jet-propelled by hope, they have paid the final tribute. They have confessed their surrender and their faith.

In spite of its enchantments, *Peter Pan* has always been a fantasy which would have been strengthened had Philip Wylie been called in for a few last-minute revisions. It is as mother-ridden as Barrie's own life.

Arnold Bennett had the perception to realize this long ago. He had first seen *Peter Pan* in 1906. In his *Journal* he then described it as possessing "sheer genius." He even went so far as to hail it "as the finest modern work for the English stage." But in 1924 when he attended a revival, though he still found it "full of the most charming fancy and invention, and often very true to life," Bennett noted that "it isn't about P.P. and not growing up, it's all about the mother-theme, with which Barrie must have been greatly preoccupied when he wrote it. The real mother dominates the first and last acts (in particular, last scene but two and last scene but one). In the other acts Wendy plays at being a mother and P.P. at being a father. Everyone wants to be mothered—even Smee—except the braves and some of the pirates. The play is simply all mothering. Even the dog is a mother-nurse."

What Freud or Sir Henry Harcourt-Reilly in *The Cocktail Party* would have made of Barrie's lifelong affair with his mother, Margaret Ogilvy, we have fortunately been spared. Nonetheless Barrie, the eternal child, did grow and keep on growing, after *Peter Pan*. He never grew up, at least in the ordinary sense. To the end he found it hard to put childish things behind him. Even the pipe upon which the author of *My Lady Nicotine* puffed seemed more happily employed, as Beerbohm suggested, when releasing soap bubbles than when used for smoking.

But Barrie was, of course, more than a child, with a child's unworldly sense of wonder and a child's capacity to believe wholeheartedly in the unreal. There was also something spinsterish about his spirit, something sacheted and tearily tender, something soft and satiny, as given to old lavender as it was to cream puffs and caramels. Often he appeared to approach the fraternity of men through sorority doors. His winsomeness could be so intolerable and his sweetness so curdling that it is easy to understand the widespread allergy to Barrie which has developed over the years.

Take his stage directions, for example. They can be more elfin than a forest full of Brownies. Their cuteness can send the stoutest stomachs spinning. A few unfortunate illustrations, chosen at random, will suffice. Let us start with Peter Pan's entrance. "Then the window is blown open, probably by the smallest and therefore most mischievous star, and Peter Pan flies into the room." Or consider John Shand's first appearance in *What Every Woman Knows*. "The window opens and shuts as softly as if this were a mother peering in to see whether her baby is asleep." Or take the sentence in *A Kiss for Cinderella* which says Mr. Bodie "is a painter for the nicest of reasons, that it is delightful to live and die in a messy studio; for our part, we too should have become a painter had it not been that we always lost our paint-box."

Turn next to *Quality Street* and what do we find? "There seems no sufficient reason," writes Barrie, "why we should choose Miss Phoebe as our heroine rather than any of the others, except, perhaps, that we like her name best. But we gave her the name, so we must support our choice and say that she is slightly the nicest, unless, indeed, Miss Susan is nicer." As a final test of the reader's patience and my own dramamine supply, let me quote from *The Old Lady Shows Her Medals*. Four London charwomen are discovered at the tea table. "As you can see by their everyday garments, and by their pails and mops (which are having a little tea-party by themselves in the corner), it is not a gathering by invitations stretching away into yesterday, it is a purely informal affair; so much more attractive, don't you think? than banquets elaborately prearranged." No wonder that, when asked to swallow such syrup, George Jean Nathan insisted that Barrie represented the triumph of sugar over diabetes.

Barrie was well aware that his writings could get beyond his control. At St. Andrews, in a famous passage, he let the cat out of the bag. With typical whimsicality he gave the name of M'Connachie to the unruly half of himself: the writing half. "I am the half that is dour and practical and canny, he is the fanciful half," said Barrie; "my desire is to be the family solicitor, standing firm on my hearthrug among the harsh realities of the office furniture; while he prefers to fly around on one wing. I should not mind him doing that, but he drags me with him."

It is because M'Connachie, the one-winged sprite, does drag

Barrie around with him that some of us have developed so hearty a dislike for M'Connachie. He is the real villain in Barrie's works, the destroyer of Barrie's virtues, the seducer he could not resist. He, I am certain, wrote the regrettable stage directions already referred to. Although Barrie might insist "M'Connachie is the one who writes the plays," I prefer to hold him responsible for writing what is bad in them; for mistaking lollipops for language, treacle for thought, and persuading Barrie again and again that mica was gold.

"Beware of M'Connachie," was Barrie's advice at St. Andrews. He added, "When I look in a mirror now it is his face I see. I speak with his voice. I once had a voice of my own, but nowadays I hear it from far away only, a melancholy, lonely, lost little pipe. I wanted to be an explorer, but he willed otherwise. You will all have your M'Connachies luring you off the high road. Unless you are constantly on the watch, you will find that he has slowly pushed you out of yourself and taken your place. He has rather done for me."

Indeed he had. Barrie was conscious of his own limitations. He resented the fact that he was his own Sentimental Tommy. He realized, as he put it, that he was "battered by the neglect of sex." He cringed when anyone was shabby enough to tag him as whimsical or elusive. He wanted to be described as "the Inoffensive Barrie." By his own confession he always thought of himself as being rather realistic. He wished that sentiment had been left out of him.

With a smiling sadness characteristic of him, he contended on one occasion that Richard Coeur de Lion was the character in history he most closely resembled. Barrie liked to picture himself as a lion. "Have you ever seen a lion at the zoo unable to chase from his cage a mob of sparrows?" he asked at a public dinner. "I have sometimes thought that children and fairies are my sparrows, and that I am the badgered lion. [As for children and fairies] . . . I could never abide them."

"If only I could write something harmful!" he sighed. But he could not. What he wrote at his best in *Dear Brutus*, *The Admirable Crichton*, *What Every Woman Knows*, or *Peter Pan* was far more than merely virtuous. When M'Connachie was under control, it was, of course, charming and whimsical. It was as full of Barrieisms as John Shand's speeches were of those Shandyisms which Maggie supplied. Yet it was also wise with the wisdom which comes from knowing that reality is not confined to appearance or facts and that, though two and two should make four on the blackboard, they can make three or one or twenty in the human heart.

Under the dew of the Barrie mist was a Scotch thistle. The courageous was there no less than the soft, the strong along with the sentimental. Barrie really believed in the good, the true, and the beautiful. "The laugh that children are born with lasts just so long as they have perfect faith," Dearth could say to his Dream Daughter in *Dear Brutus*. Barrie never lost that faith or that laugh.

Surely a man thus blessed is not entirely ready for the oubliette in a world where faith is shrinking and facts grow uglier. The better half of Barrie—the half he ruled himself—is worth saving. If no longer in the theatre, then certainly in movies, British made, and with all the constables in the kingdom on hand to keep M'Connachie, that unbearable wretch, off the lots.

May 13 *and* 20, 1950

THE STORY behind the creation of Stevenson's "fine bogey tale," as told in an introduction for a new edition of Dr. Jekyll and Mr. Hyde *issued by the Limited Editions Club and the Heritage Press.*

꒰꒱꒰꒱꒰꒱꒰꒱꒰꒱꒰꒱꒰꒱꒰꒱꒰꒱꒰꒱꒰꒱꒰꒱꒰꒱꒰꒱꒰꒱꒰꒱꒰꒱

R.L.S. and "Dr. Jekyll"

WHEN Stevenson arrived in America in 1887, things were not at all as they had been eight summers earlier. Dr. Jekyll could not have been more different from Mr. Hyde. As a matter of fact, it was *Dr. Jekyll and Mr. Hyde* which more than anything else was responsible for the change.

At the time of his first visit no one had met Stevenson at the pier. He was friendless in New York, and he came alone. His most tangible asset was hope and the consciousness, as he put it, that "there is something in me worth saying, though I can't find what it is just yet." He was then an author little known and so hard up that on the *Devonia* he had exposed himself to all the discomforts of traveling steerage. If he spent a single night in the city, and that at a shilling boarding house at 10 West Street, his reasons, both personal and professional, for saving money were urgent. He was a free-lance writer, trying for once to make a go of it on his own without any financial aid from his father. His need was copy, his quest more romantic.

News from Fanny Osbourne had summoned him to California. Fanny was, of course, the American woman who was to play so large a part in his life, his writing, and those incessant odysseys in search of health which finally took him to Samoa. Stevenson had met her three years before at Fontainebleau when, to escape from an unhappy marriage, she was living in France with her son and daughter. The fact that she was eleven years his senior had not kept him from falling in love with her at once. The news from Fanny, bad and good, was sufficient to make him, in spite of his own precarious health, brave even the hardships of an immigrant train across the country on his long trek to San Francisco. For he had heard that Fanny was ill, seriously ill. And she had written that she might at last be granted a divorce.

All this was in 1879. Stevenson's arrival on September 7, 1887, was quite another thing. Only the old struggle with illness remained the same. Stevenson's father had died the previous spring, thus breaking his son's last binding link with the British Isles which he was never to see again. Mrs. Osbourne was by now Mrs. Stevenson. Stevenson was accompanied this time by a sizable entourage—Fanny, his stepson Lloyd Osbourne, his mother, and a servant. Moreover, reporters were on hand to meet him. He was not able to see them until the next day, because a cold, caught off the Banks, necessitated his being rushed off to his hotel, the Victoria. But they were there, with all that their presence meant.

His old friend W. H. Low, the artist who was to write about Stevenson so charmingly in *A Chronicle of Friendships*, was also at the boat. A host of new friends, or of people who hoped to become his friends, was ready to make much of him. Saint-Gaudens was eager to have Stevenson sit for him. Publishers, including *Scribner's Magazine*, were on his trail with dizzying offers. The truth is that, though he found the experience "a bore and a fraud" and also very pleasant, Stevenson had become "quite a famous party" between his first and second visits to America. With reason, too.

The years 1884 to 1887 had been pivotal ones for him. They had marked the turning point in his career. During them he had ceased to be the author of well-received though generally unread travel sketches, essays, and narratives short or long, and become an international figure. His three years in England at Bournemouth had been extraordinarily productive. In spite of frequent hemorrhages and long, irksome periods in bed, he had managed to see through the presses such works as *A Child's Garden of Verses*, *Prince Otto*, *The Body Snatchers*, *More New Arabian Nights*, *Strange Case of Dr. Jekyll and Mr. Hyde*, *Kidnapped*, and *Underwoods*. A reputation slowly gained had suddenly begun to spread like an epidemic.

The true alteration in Stevenson's fortunes should have come in 1881. Then it was that over the signature of "Captain George North" a buccaneering tale of his had been serialized in a magazine called *Young Folks*, where, believe it or not, it had passed unnoted except by a few readers who wrote in scoffing letters. Two years later it had appeared in book form as *Treasure Island*, and the Stevenson boom was on.

Although Jim Hawkins's story sold no more than 5,600 copies in England during its first season, it had won its ardent and important devotees. Andrew Lang had written the author ecstatically, "I don't know, except *Tom Sawyer* and the *Odyssey*, that I have liked any romance so well." The editor of London's *Saturday Review* had confessed he thought *Treasure Island* was the best book since *Robinson Crusoe*. Even Mr. Gladstone was rumored to have thumbed the novel at Lord Rosebery's and to have spent the next day searching London for a secondhand copy of it. But famous as *Treasure Island* and these other works, especially *Kidnapped,* had made Stevenson, it was the *Strange Case of Dr. Jekyll and Mr. Hyde* which in both England and America had done the most to establish his reputation.

The story of its writing, publication, and reception is in itself an unusual tale. Every reader of poetry remembers with resentment that regrettable figure known only (and mercifully) as "a person on business from Porlock." His fate was to bring *Kubla Khan* to a full stop by calling on Coleridge at the precious moments when he was struggling to commit to paper those magical verses which had formed in his mind during the course of a three-hours' sleep induced by an anodyne. *Dr. Jekyll and Mr. Hyde* was dream-born too, but in its case interrupted in the very act of dreaming. Born of a dream? No. Of a nightmare, of course.

It was Mrs. Stevenson who, by functioning somewhat in the manner of that person from Porlock, came near to undoing the story she was afterwards to do much to help. Stevenson was having one of his bouts with illness at Bournemouth when one night during a restless sleep his cries of horror caused Mrs. Stevenson to waken him. He did not hide his irritation. "I was dreaming a fine bogey tale," said he reproachfully. Whereupon he rapidly sketched in *Dr. Jekyll and Mr. Hyde* up to the transformation scene at which point he had been awakened.

Dreams were no new experience for Stevenson. He had been "an ardent and uncomfortable dreamer" since his sickly childhood. As a boy, when he had a touch of fever he had fought in vain against the "night-hag" who would sooner or later "have him by the throat, and pluck him, strangling and screaming, from his sleep." With the passing years Stevenson's dreams had lessened in their horrors. He would wake up, he tells us in *A Chapter on Dreams,* "with no more extreme symptom than a flying heart, a freezing scalp, cold sweats, and the speechless midnight fear."

Later on when he had become a professional writer, with "bankruptcy at his heels" and the butcher lingering at the back gate, Stevenson found that dreaming had for him become a business. He had his names for the agents of his dreams even as Barrie had for M'Connachie, his whimsical *alter ego* and writing self. Stevenson referred to these agents, it pains me to admit, as "the little people" and "the Brownies." His hope was that they would supply him with marketable tales. However ghoulish they may have been as Brownies, no one can deny that they were invaluable collaborators when they worked with him on the *Strange Case of Dr. Jekyll and Mr. Hyde,* after Stevenson had wandered about for two days racking his brains "for a plot of any sort."

For some years Stevenson had been frightening himself and others by writing such tales of terror ("crawlers" he called them) as *Thrawn Janet, The Body Snatchers,* and *Markheim.* Moreover, he had long been concerned with the strange duality of human character. He had come closest to dealing with this subject in *Deacon Brodie,* that play about a man who was good by day and evil by night which he had written with W. E. Henley. But the result did not satisfy him. He was still search-ing for the right story to express "that strong sense of a man's double being which must at times come in upon him and over-whelm the mind of every thinking creature," when he dreamed the dream which so possessed him that he started writing fever-ishly at daybreak.

Stevenson said his nightmare supplied him with "the scene

at the window, and a scene afterwards split in two, in which Hyde, pursued for some crime, took the powder and underwent the change in the presence of his pursuers." He does not, however, reveal the details of the writing of *Dr. Jekyll and Mr. Hyde*, and these are exciting in their own way. A first draft of approximately thirty thousand words was dashed off in three days and read aloud to the family. Thereafter, when Stevenson had returned to his bedroom, Mrs. Stevenson wrote a detailed criticism in which, among other objections, she contended that he had sacrificed the allegory for "magnificent sensationalism." She took this criticism up to her husband and left it with him. After a while Stevenson's bell rang and Fanny is said to have found him sitting up in bed, a thermometer in his mouth, pointing to a pile of ashes in the grate. Since he was an author, his egotism was doubtless wounded. Yet he must have felt Fanny was right, because he destroyed his first draft so as to avoid the temptation of relying on it when making a fresh start.

Regardless of how he may have felt, one thing is certain. Stevenson set to work again at once, writing as swiftly as before and with the same fevered intensity. Three days later he emerged with another version of thirty thousand words. The feat he had performed was prodigious. For a healthy author to turn out sixty thousand words in six days would be incredible enough; for an invalid such as Stevenson it was miraculous. Instead of exhausting him, he was apparently exhilarated by the effort.

When the manuscript was revised it was sent to *Longmans Magazine*, where the editorial decision was to publish it as a shilling book rather than to break it up into monthly sections. The small volume came from the presses at just the wrong time. The book stores, already overloaded with their Christmas stock, would not touch it. It was withheld until January, and then launched with difficulty. No one boosted it and few bought it until an enticing notice appeared in the London *Times*. Then suddenly it began to catch on, and within the next six months nearly forty thousand copies were sold in England alone.

Its sale in the United States was no less impressive (in pirated versions as well as the authorized edition); its impact equally spectacular. Ministers preached about it, religious journals devoted long articles to it, and laymen gulped it down (even as you and I still do), giving it their warm approval because it froze their blood. The *Strange Case of Dr. Jekyll and Mr. Hyde* did more than find its way into the hands of unexpected readers. It entered the theatre, too. In fact, five nights after Stevenson's arrival Richard Mansfield scored one of his outstanding successes in a dramatization of it by T. R. Sullivan, though Stevenson missed the performance because his illness forced him to flee to Newport with some old friends for a rest. The truest measure of the story's popularity was that the names in its title had already passed into the language, where they have remained ever since as synonyms for good and evil and a split personality. Its author had amusing proof of this the day before the *Ludgate Hill* reached New York. When the pilot, evidently a hateful man, came aboard Stevenson must have been pleased and staggered to learn that the crew referred to him as Hyde, while his amiable partner was known as Jekyll.

It must be remembered, as many have pointed out, that the *Strange Case of Dr. Jekyll and Mr. Hyde* appeared years before Freud or Jung or Adler had explored the shadowy recesses of the mind, the dark realm of the subconscious, and the conflicting traits and impulses which (as everyone nowadays recognizes) torture men and women, not by neatly halving them in the Jekyll-Hyde fashion, but by subdividing them into endless overlapping claims. We have long since come to admit the plurality of man's nature, rather than its duality. Nonetheless, psychoanalysis cannot wither nor psychiatry stale the fascination and the horror of the expedition on which Stevenson leads us through the terrifying underworld of character.

Stevenson must have been aware of the plurality of his own nature. The man who in a first draft could write, "The world is so great and I am so small/I do not like it at all, at all," and then revise this to read, "The world is so full of a number of things/I am sure we should all be as happy as kings," was certainly not a person to whom contradictions were unknown. The fact that such contradictions abounded in Stevenson enriched not only his writing but his personality.

Stevenson was an escaped or—and here was a source of torture—an almost-escaped Calvinist who had turned Bohemian. Although he had more than the average male's courage, he remained something of a boy-man until he died at the age of forty-four. He was a bookish fellow and an invalid who, in spite of being often forced to live as a prisoner in "the land of counterpane," loved the out-of-doors with an athlete's relish. He was a writer (and a fine one) who, had he been able to choose his endowments, might have been a man of action. Most of those privileged to meet him were captivated by him. But, delightful and ebullient as he was, his indignation could be blistering, as everyone knows who has ever been stirred by his rousing defense of Father Damien in that open letter he sent at the risk of a libel suit to a minister he thought villainous, a man whose name just happened to be Hyde.

If there was a considerable amount of the actor in Stevenson, there was even more of the preacher. In addition to being stagestruck, he remained as a grown-up a person who preferred to see the world in the violent terms of Skelt, that designer of toy theatres who had nourished his youthful dreams. Skeltery, however, could not blind Stevenson to the truth any more than the Ariel, Puck, and Antony aspects of his nature could keep him from being, in Henley's phrase, "Hamlet most of all." The serenity, the confidence, even the innocence popularly associated with his name tend to obscure the inner disturbances of his spirit which were no less real.

Stevenson was far from being the uncomplicated person that *A Child's Garden of Verses, Treasure Island, Kidnapped, Lay Morals,* or his famous *Requiem* might lead one to believe. If he could as an adult invite his young readers with an infant's purity to "go up in a swing/Up in the air so blue," he could also force his contemporaries to look upon the head of the Medusa. That he was a good man, warm-hearted, generous, and even noble, no one could deny. But surely few men so good have ever shown so doting an affection for murder, violence, corpses, bloodshed, pain, and the black, intrusive mysteries of the night, or had a greater preoccupation with evil.

If I dwell on these inconsistencies in Stevenson the man, it is because I believe we have them to thank for his astonishing understanding of the duality of the good Dr. Jekyll whose other self took the form of Mr. Hyde. His long short story remains in a class by itself. It is a *tour de force* of amazing virtuosity. Whatever his deficiencies may have been in the sustained novel meant for adult consumption, Stevenson was as a prose artist one of the most adroit technicians ever to have employed the English language.

Critics have pointed out (making an exception, of course, of the unfinished *Weir of Hermiston* with its magnificent proofs of its author's having come fully into his own at last) that Stevenson as a novelist was, because of his poor health and quickly expended energies, a writer of brilliant beginnings. The *Strange Case of Dr. Jekyll and Mr. Hyde* is short enough to have left his creative powers unexhausted. It may suffer technically by having both Dr. Lanyon and Dr. Jekyll tell their stories in a style as impeccable as Stevenson's own. But the narrative is built and advanced with a marvelous awareness of every thrill and shudder its gruesome tale contains. It is melo-drama, sulphurous and appalling, which by the sheer black magic of its telling is lifted into literature.

A test of any book's quality is the extent to which it can sur-vive rereading. This is particularly true of thrillers which, as a rule, have suspense, and only suspense, as their ally. What happens is all we want to know. The manner of the telling is apt to be of scant interest and to offer no satisfactions of its own. In the instance of *Dr. Jekyll and Mr. Hyde* the telling is as exciting as the tale. I have read it uncountable times and never without having my hair stand "upon my head like quills," to borrow Stevenson's phrase. Instead of diminishing, my admira-tion has grown with each rereading.

Although it has its serious and frightening overtones which explain the percussive effect it creates even now, it is first and foremost a spine-twister meant to be gobbled up as such. The persons to be most envied are, of course, those coming to it for the first time. Nonetheless, the repeaters are not to be pitied. They, too, are lucky ones; that is, if they care about good writ-ing, an interest which should be, though all too seldom is, one of the most compelling reasons for reading. I know I find an inexhaustible fascination in the way in which Stevenson succeeds in turning what could easily have been a penny thriller into a tale of terror which is a masterpiece of its kind.

The style in itself is a delight. The sentences have an etcher's precision. Varied as their cadences are and eerie as is the music they create, they drive on steadily with ever mounting tension as they unfold their terrible story. Darkness, brilliantly used, is the inevitable background for the black secrets and blacker crimes of Mr. Hyde—"the gross darkness of the night." The moon appearing suddenly to cast its pale light on murder. Murky side streets with their muddy ways. The midnight striking of clocks. Or by day a chocolate-colored London fog muffling and smothering the city, and enveloping it like a pall. These are some of the means by which the stage is set with words.

Stevenson is no less skilful in starting his story. Two men as different as Mr. Utterson and Mr. Enfield lead us into this tale about a dual personality. The contrast between them is the first of many to come. It is an oblique preparation for those violent contrasts in size, age, looks, emotions, manners, desires, and deeds which separate the admired and benevolent Dr. Jekyll from his odious *alter ego*.

Familiar as I am with them, I never cease to marvel at the clues Stevenson gives, little by little, to solve the mystery of Jekyll and Hyde and to suggest their oneness. The signature on the check, the walking stick, the letter no one delivered, the testimony of the clerk who was expert at handwriting, Poole's report, the face at the window, the changed Dr. Jekyll, the disappearance of Hyde after the murder of Sir Danvers Carew, and the missing medicine. With such hints, dropped at the most strategic intervals, Stevenson plays hare-and-hounds with horror.

I doubt if even Richard III is described in terms more loathsome than those applied to Mr. Hyde. At first he is defined for us only by the emotions he creates in others. We learn of Mr. Enfield's instantaneous hatred of him; of the desire to kill him that turns a doctor sick and white; and of the murderous anger of the women in the street. We feel him before we see him, and come to dread seeing him. Thereupon Mr. Enfield attempts to describe the sense he creates of there being something wrong about him, something displeasing, downright detestable and deformed. From then on, the words applied to Hyde are hideous and horrible as he is. He is troglodytic. Satan's signature is upon his face. He is ape-like, wicked-looking, monkey-like, a rat, shocking, abnormal, and misbegotten. He is all these things—and more.

Beastly as we know Hyde to be, we see him commit only one murder. Yet he haunts our minds as a mass murderer. He is a man whose pleasure is pain and whose villainies are incessant. He is, in short, pure evil, and that is the only purity he knows. Dr. Jekyll's is the final life he takes. This is Jekyll's penalty for having summoned and released him.

In Samoa Stevenson was known as Tusitala, the teller of tales. He never told a better tale of horror than the *Strange Case of Dr. Jekyll and Mr. Hyde* or one that found and has continued to hold so large a public. A "crawler" it may be, but it is a "crawler" with wings.

December 1 and 8, 1951

A YEAR of New York living as seen, felt, thought, and phrased by Brooks Atkinson, that uncommon man—a person wise enough to accept the universe on its own terms.

≋≋≋≋≋≋≋≋≋≋≋≋≋≋≋≋≋≋≋≋≋≋≋≋≋≋≋≋≋≋

Manhattan's Thoreau

THIRTY YEARS ago Brooks Atkinson, then an assistant to H. T. Parker on the *Boston Transcript*, reviewed a Harvard Dramatic Club production of François Coppée's four-character play, *The Violins of Cremona*. Although he had nice things to say about three of the four undergraduate actors, the rest of the cast, he concluded, "sputtered and spurted." As I happened to be the rest of the cast, I have been reading Mr. Atkinson with increasing pleasure ever since.

I have known him as a friend for more than a quarter of a century. I have marveled at the felicity, wisdom, and perception of his dramatic criticism in *The New York Times* these many years. I have followed with pride his war career as a correspondent, first at Chungking and then at Moscow, which won him the Pulitzer Prize for Journalism in 1947. I have read his fine essays on Thoreau and Emerson, those fellow Yankees whose spirit he shares. And devoured all of his books from *Skyline Promenades, Henry Thoreau, Cosmic Yankee,* and *East of the Hudson* to *The Cingalese Prince* and *Broadway Scrapbook*. Yet even now I find myself sputtering and spurting again when I try to suggest the dimension and the

quality of the man who emerges from the pages of Mr. Atkinson's newest volume, *Once Around the Sun.**

Mr. Atkinson's is a very personal book. Although this is what
all books should be and all good ones are, books that are signed
by their authors in almost every sentence are rarer than one
might think. All too many books could have been written by
any number of people. They spill from a kind of Willow Run
of competence and possess no individual color or flavor. They
speak to others without speaking for the men who wrote them.
Everything is in them except their authors.

One of the beckoning virtues of *Once Around the Sun* is
that Mr. Atkinson and only Mr. Atkinson could have felt and
thought and phrased it. His diary of a year's living is as inti-
mate as a late evening's talk with him or a walk along Manhattan's bustling waterfront or a visit in the country. It is more
revealing than such sharings of his mind and insights, his hopes
and hobbies, could hope to be because, luckily, no one is present
to interrupt him. What he has to say concisely and eloquently,
with a shining honesty and directness, merits more than passing
attention. It deserves underscoring, rereading, and reflection.
It is the kind of comment on countless subjects that one wants
to go back to, fearful of forgetting, anxious to absorb.

The census takers tell us there are more than eight million
people living (or existing) in New York City. I feel safe in
wagering that among all those millions there is not a single
person quite like Mr. Atkinson. Or one who, in his phrase,
"practises mortality" in his fashion on this overcrowded island.
He manages to resist the stampede of the herd and remain an
individual in the midst of a mob. His only eccentricity is his

* *Once Around the Sun,* by Brooks Atkinson. New York: Harcourt, Brace
& Co. 376 pp. $4.

sanity; his only oddity is that, surrounded by so many who are frantic or rudderless, he continues to be calm and to follow his own course.

Though no one has spoken more discerningly about living in New York than Mr. Atkinson, he is not the typical Manhattanite. Plainly he is not by temperament the cigarette type. He exudes the mythical placidity of the pipe-smoker. His very appearance makes clear that he is blessed with a philosopher's serenity. Although his fellow aisle-sitters have been gradually battered by the calendar, Mr. Atkinson has somehow eluded its blows.

His face is singularly free of those fretful creases, puffs, and saggings which mark a troubled man's erosion. His mustache may have some gray in it, but his hair, which admits no open spaces, is an unworried black. His grayish-blue eyes are wonderfully clear. They are as quick to reflect thoughts or humor as they are to catch the markings and contours of a hermit thrush or a Henslow's sparrow. Mr. Atkinson never seems to be in a hurry even when scurrying up an aisle to meet a midnight deadline or pushing his way through Broadway crowds to reach his desk at the *Times*. Although his body is slight and wiry, his photographs tell the real truth about him by making him look larger than he is—except in spirit. It is not often that the smiling, lusty stuffs of gaiety and the good, solid granite of character (not to forget a capacity for exaltation) are so mixed in one person.

Did Diogenes search for an honest man? He would have found one in Mr. Atkinson. He is one person in an age cursed with neuroses, fears, surrenders, and complexes, who seems complicated (if not unbelievable) only because he has not lost his simplicity. He is the least slick city-slicker imaginable. He is a summer farmer who carries the country with him into Cosmopolis and finds nature thriving there in spite of bricks and asphalt. New York with all its pressures has been unable to corrupt him.

He is a sophisticate in a larger sense of the word than urban cliff-dwellers understand. Though an omnivorous reader and an incessant and untiring playgoer, his cultivation does not stop with books or plays. Life is his province. Not cocktail-party life, which he despises; nor café society homelessness and exhibitionism; nor white-collar conformity; nor life as it trickles into those eddies known as literary cliques. No, not any of these. But life in war-torn China or Russia, life on his farm, life on New York's streets and piers, wild life and the seasonal changes of nature, life wherever the sun shines and the human spirit is tested.

Mr. Atkinson is a follower of Thoreau whose odd choice for a Walden Pond has been Manhattan. Although the theatre may be his profession and one at which he excels, no make-believe can blind him to reality. Arcturus, Sirius, and Procyon are stars that he watches with perhaps greater affection than he does those twinkling on Broadway. His contention is that "in the ideal sense nothing is uninteresting; there are only uninterested people." Count Mr. Atkinson among the lucky ones, the passionately interested. Count him among those (and they are rare) who have a genius for full living; who can immerse themselves in what each day offers and are tinglingly aware of what goes on around them.

Small things no less than large concern him. The character of his neighbors, the sights and sounds of Manhattan, history made and history in the making, the glories and the shams of art, the possibilities of man's being and becoming, "the root and muscle of America," "the fundamentals of human activity"—all these and many more are among the absorptions which, because they enliven his life, have found their way into his book.

What holds a special fascination for Mr. Atkinson? The Hudson, the "mature river . . . benign as well as beautiful," upon which his apartment faces. Every freighter and steamer that travels its tranquil waters linking New York with the far reaches of the earth. Birds, keenly observed and charmingly written about; birds individualized and yet seen as spokesmen for cosmic forces. The changing stars, and for the same reason. Gardens. His farm. His friends. New York's bad living but electric thinking.

Its skyscrapers trying not to see the dirt on the pavements below them. His job, which he loves, and the *Times,* which he also loves, and the schedule of night work and daytime wanderings which they make possible. Newspapers, especially on long quiet evenings when hours can be squandered poking into their "savory corners" for the tidbits of news. Writing, preferably "plain writing by men who have had experiences outside the library"; above all, clear writing. The therapy of such manual labor as painting a barn or building a bathroom cabinet. Election Day, which Mr. Atkinson thinks he enjoys more than any other day. His work as a Grand Juror. Or Thursday, the brightest day of each week because it brings the "incomparable" *New Yorker.*

In *Once Around the Sun* Mr. Atkinson has his many entries for the birthdays of such men as Thomas Paine, Jackson, Jefferson, Whitman, Audubon, Thoreau, and Melville; for such anniversaries as the *Clermont*'s sailing, the signing of the U.N. Charter, Pearl Harbor, Washington's inauguration, and the unveiling of the Statue of Liberty; and for such holidays as Christmas, Thanksgiving, Yom Kippur, and May Day (when local Communists and those in Russia like "arctic lemmings . . . are marching to their own destruction"). These commemorative essays provoke Mr. Atkinson into little gems of biography, political comment, observations of inspired common sense, or paragraphs sweetened with philosophy. They find him once again, as with ships, birds, or stars, looking for the inter-relationship between things; in this case, between the past and the present.

When asked to define his religious beliefs, Mr. Atkinson falls back on that almost forgotten New England word "Transcendentalist." Transcendentalism, says he, was "basically a religious philosophy that saw God . . . here and now in the midst of the workaday world, the animating force behind every creative impulse. . . . I like the warmth, brightness, confidence, and hope of the transcendentalist universe in which I am related to all men and all growing things and am not shut off from anything except by my own ignorance or the feebleness of my own vitality."

This may come close to stating Mr. Atkinson's philosophy. It may explain why he so resolutely believes with Emerson in the "infinitude of the private man." It may be the key to his proper distrust of pure intellect, his conviction that "culture should include the whole man," and his insistence that "books are not primary sources" since "there is no substitute for people." But it does not give us the whole Atkinson. It does not cover the cracker-barrel sage with a gift for poetic phrasing who knows "it is better to win a war than to lose it, but not much better"; and who is aware that, since the government is composed of people, it can be only as good as average people. Nor does it take into account Mr. Atkinson's chuckling and warm sense of humor. "Trust only the men who laugh with relish," he advises. Then he admits, "I trust Shakespeare more than Corneille, Mark Twain more than Henry James, Robert Frost more than T. S. Eliot, Ernest Hemingway more than Thomas Mann. They do not expect to vanquish folly from the world overnight."

I hope I have in no way done Mr. Atkinson the injustice of painting him as an unthinking optimist. But neither is he a pessimist of the whining variety that finds pleasure in pain. He just happens to see life plain, to face it unafraid, and to live it (as he says of the young sea-going Melville) with the exaltation of a man who has joined the universe on its own terms. He has no longing for the good old days. He finds the present engrossing if for no other reason than that he has survived and absorbed the horrors of the modern world undaunted. He knows the average man well enough to place his faith in him, no matter how much governments may blunder or international events discourage him. It is not surprising that twice he commends famous men for their "moral grandeur." Moral grandeur is something Mr. Atkinson himself possesses. One reason he is so fine a writer is that he is so fine a man.

August 11, 1951

CHAS ADDAMS'S realm of bats, broomsticks, glamour-ghouls, and blood-letting morons, which contributes to the world's delight by adding to its horrors.

🐜🐜🐜🐜🐜🐜🐜🐜🐜🐜🐜🐜🐜🐜🐜🐜🐜🐜🐜🐜🐜🐜🐜🐜🐜🐜🐜🐜🐜🐜🐜🐜🐜🐜

Welcome Monsters

*D*EAREST: *How I wish you were here with me now to see how lovely our little garden has become! The black nightshade is in full bloom, and the death camass we planted last fall is coming along beautifully. The henbane seems to have shot up overnight. You will be glad to know that the dwarf's hair was not affected by the dry spell, as we feared, after all. A myriad of delightful little slugs have appeared, as if from nowhere, on the rotten stump by the belladonna patch, and this morning I noticed snake eggs hatching near the pool. Do finish up that business, darling, and hurry home.*

Plainly this is not a letter dashed off by any ordinary green-thumbed wife to any ordinary husband who happens to share her interest in gardening. It is a note which one and only one woman could have written, and which one and only one person, her creator, would have thought of having her write in quite such a way with just such a calm absorption in the stuffs of mid-night, sorcery, poison, and decay.

The woman, of course, is that glamour-ghoul, the lanky young witch with the chalk-white skin and the hearse-black gown and locks, who is everyone's joy whenever she haunts the pages of *The New Yorker*. Her creator, need it be said, is

· 45 ·

Charles Addams; the same and utterly unique Mr. Addams whose hilarious derangements can now be relished in a collection of his cartoons inspirationally entitled *Chas Addams's MONSTER RALLY.**

Monsters, young or old, four-legged or two-headed, prehistoric or contemporary, simpering or nonchalant, are very much Mr. Addams's affair. His is a hobgoblin world of bats, spiders, broomsticks, snakes, cobwebs, and bloodletting morons in which every day is Hallowe'en. If his creatures hold life lightly and play with death as if it were a toy, it is because they are, each witch's or mother's son or daughter among them, jubilant nihilists.

They are as unburdened with consciences as they are with causes. Murder for them, regardless of their years, is something which exercises their ingenuity as planners without involving their emotions as people. They are Mr. Hydes untroubled by Dr. Jekylls. A teacher is no more appalled by erasing a sentence from the blackboard than they are by doing away with a husband, a wife, themselves, or the little girl next door. They do not kill to liberate anything except their own perversity or to express their disregard for the human race to which, in its average manifestations, they plainly do not belong.

A key to an understanding of this new Addams tribe (so different from the one "d'd" New England family) is to be found in a drawing in *Monster Rally* which shows an audience composed of even-as-you-and-I mortals watching a movie. What they are seeing we can see by looking at them. Many of the women, some of the men, too, have tears splashing down their cheeks. Every face is taut with pity or terror. More accurately,

* *Monster Rally*, by Chas Addams. With an introduction by John O'Hara. New York: Simon & Schuster. 91 pp. $2.95.

every face is responding in the normal, hence expected, way except one. This is the moon-white, moon-round mug of that baldheaded, eyebrowless, bug-eyed, snaggle-toothed, sausage-nosed old cretin who has somehow wandered into this convention of humdrum, everyday citizens as Mr. Addams's delegate. And what is he doing, this amoral, slug-brained, icicle-hearted moron? Laughing, of course. Laughing openly, deliriously. Laughing as all of us countless thousands of Chas Addams fans (who at least try to be good members of the Republic) howl with glee whenever ours is the pleasant privilege of seeing one of Mr. Addams's cartoons.

William Shakespeare was a fellow who shared Mr. Addams's interest in violence, gore, ghosts, and murder. He, too, had a pretty taste for witches, knew the terrors of the midnight hour, and was on speaking terms with death. But the man from Stratford, though a genius, was run-of-the-mill enough to take a serious thing seriously. When his Macduff, for example, returned from inspecting the bloody remains of old King Duncan, he was not in a laughing mood. "Horror! horror! horror! Tongue nor heart/Cannot conceive nor name thee!" he cried in somewhat fancier terms than we would use, though expressing the feelings all of us would have were we to be confronted by the same or a similar sight.

Mr. Addams, however, may I quickly add, is as different from Shakespeare as he is from Edgar Allan Poe. Nothing shocks him and no one is shocked by him. The more sinister his concepts are, the louder is our laughter and the greater our enjoyment. Clearly Mr. Addams invites us to enter a world which has nothing to do with the one in which we live except that, in the most glorious, undeviating, and giddy fashion, it turns all of its values topsy-turvy.

Most husbands, since their self-interest is involved, are inclined to frown on husband-killing wives. Most wives, for the same valid reason, are apt to regard unfondly husbands who are wife-killers. Yet all couples, however happy, are made the happier when Mr. Addams draws a wife packing her poor unsuspecting mate's lunch-box with a time-charge of dynamite. Or when he sketches a mild-seeming man who, having parked his car so that the door to the trailer in which his wife is traveling will open onto the steepest of cliffs, calls, "Oh, darling, can you step out for a moment?"

Elia's famous contention was that what made the artificial comedies of the Restoration and post-Restoration years acceptable was that they managed to get out of Christendom into a universe of their own. They were, therefore, safely beyond morality and police-court judgments. What Lamb would have made of Mr. Addams's work, I cannot guess. I do know that for those of us who dote on Mr. Addams's work, the point, the triumph, the delight of his drawings is that in their own uproarious and demented way they turn Elia's fantasy into a fact.

Mr. Addams's sense of the absurd is inexhaustible. It is not limited to his family of witches who live in their spooky and tattered ruin of an American Victorian home with their wayward offspring and those two unforgettable men, the leering defective with the Dewey mustache and the creature who out-Karloffs Boris Karloff.

Consider, for instance, the nurse who calmly pushes a pram in which some dear little monster is sleeping behind stout iron bars. Or the bride who heats a branding-iron in the living room on her wedding night while her groom unpacks in the next room. Or the irate wife who, when she finds her husband dangling from a chandelier, a chair overturned, a noose around his neck, and his left arm caught in the noose, cries with contempt, "For Heaven's sake, can't you do anything right?" Or the sick-looking cannibal who, sitting empty-handed at suppertime by a steaming caldron while his tribesmen are gobbling up their food, says plaintively, "Oh, I like missionary all right but missionary doesn't like me."

I must admit I have a special fondness for those frightening little brats, those incipient Loebs and Leopolds, who most often attract Mr. Addams's attention. I have in mind such of his bantam ogres as the two dumpling-headed kids just about to send a boulder rolling down a hill toward the fancy car in which an inoffensive motorist has his eyes fixed on a sign reading, "CAREFUL! Children at Play." Or the appalling little boy who is reaching in the medicine cabinet in his bathroom to dip an arrow into a bottle marked "Poison." Or the identical fiend when, from one side of a pond in the Park, he is aiming a toy submarine at the flotilla of toy sailboats with which more innocent children are playing. Or the same menace again when he is sending a toy school bus straight into the path of an oncoming toy train. Or when, with his sister's aid, he is guillotining a doll on Christmas day. Or standing on his bed, which has carved vultures for bedposts, to add a sign saying, "NO DIVING—Pool Empty," to his demon's collection of stolen warnings which read, "STOP—Bridge Out," "Dangerous Undertow," "Keep Clear—High Voltage," etc., etc.

Choosing a favorite among Mr. Addams's cartoons is difficult. Perhaps, however, the drawing among all Addams drawings I wish most that I owned is the memorable one in which, at Christmas time, from the tower of her Victorian home, Mr. Addams's black-haired young witch is watching the Karloff character and his half-witted friend empty a vat of steaming lye on some gentle carolers as they stand singing, full of seasonal cheer, at the front door four floors below.

Naturally (if I may use such a word in connection with Mr. Addams, whose excellence is his unnaturalness), it is fascinating to learn about the kind of man who lives with such thoughts, can think up such horrors, and provide such ghoulish pleasures. For this information I refer you to the amusing and enlightening foreword with which John O'Hara has supplied *Chas Addams's MONSTER RALLY*. I also urge you to read the longer, more detailed, and immensely diverting study of Mr. Addams's life, character, and works by John Kobler. This appears as the first chapter in *Afternoon in the Attic*, Mr. Kobler's rewarding study of eccentrics, a volume to which Mr. Addams has contributed illustrations worthy both of him and of Mr. Kobler.

Beyond dispute the age in which we live abounds in its monstrous aspects. No less surely Mr. Addams's is the paradoxical distinction of having reduced the horrors of the present by having added to them. If only the other horrors were as laughable as the ones with which he delights us!

November 11, 1950

THE FINAL indestructible fanaticism of the true artist, as Agnes de Mille has lived it and recorded it in words that make our lives "less daily."

Look, Pa, I'm Dancin'

THERE is a lightning that no one sees and that only one person feels—the person who is hit by it. Although it flashes unpredictably, it ignites without destroying. It does not speed from the skies to the earth but from age to youth, and is a matter of influence and inspiration. It strikes when a young person suddenly has his interest polarized and his life altered by chancing to come under the spell of a colorful public figure or performer who is unaware of what is happening.

This kind of lightning has struck throughout the whole of history and fortunately is striking now, though where and how the world does not know. It struck in London one evening in the early Eighties when a tall, reedy Irishman named George Bernard Shaw, who had not hitherto been interested in economics or political science, wandered into a hall and heard an American, Henry George, talk on Land Nationalization and the Single Tax. That speech by the author of *Progress and Poverty*, Shaw later confessed, "changed the whole current of my life."

Some forty years later, halfway around the world in Los Angeles, a girl of thirteen was struck by this same lightning which is always ready to strike the lucky. The girl was Agnes de Mille, the granddaughter of Henry George. She had been taken by her mother to see Pavlova. A birdlike creature, all wonder and fascination and lightness, filled the stage with glory and the child with ecstasy.

As she watched Pavlova dance, the blood beat in the girl's throat. When Pavlova jumped, her spirit soared even as Pavlova's body seemed to fly. She had never imagined such grace and was seldom again to know a like excitement. She had been led into a realm of dreams and enchantment. She had witnessed "the power of beauty." Her head ached with happiness as she left the theatre. She could not talk and did not wish to cry. She had had an experience which, in her words, burned in a single afternoon a path over which she could never retrace her steps. As she puts it in her autobiography, "My life was wholly altered by her."

How many lives have been and will be altered by Miss de Mille's *Dance to the Piper*,* there is no way of telling. Certainly some will be, because hers is more than an engrossing book. It is a needed book, welcome and exciting. Although its subject is the world of the dance, its interest is not limited to those who follow that world or care about it.

It has much to say to everyone practising or responsive to any of the arts, for the lightning of inspiration is in it. It changes us as we read it by making us feel "less daily," to borrow Miss de Mille's fine phrase for the effect Pavlova had on her audiences. The wonder, the heartbreak, the intensity, the drudgery, the hardship, the hoping and fearing, the joy and agony, the dedication, the martyrdom, and the glory of the true artist's life are laid bare in its pages with humor and gal-

* *Dance to the Piper*, by Agnes de Mille. Boston: Little, Brown and Co. An Atlantic Monthly Press book. 342 pp. $3.50.

lantry, and with a skill so exceptional that professional authors would have every reason to resent the brilliance of the writing if their admiration did not silence their envy.

Quite aside from the rich enjoyment it provides, Miss de Mille's autobiography has an importance which cannot be overstressed, particularly at present. Arts and the artist have had a hard time in the contemporary world. For far too many years man has had to be preoccupied with other concerns. Grave problems of economics, the passions of politics, the tensions of international crises, the threats or horrors of war, and the fears of the atomic age have commanded his attention and drained his energies. In an age of crisis a literature of brutality and toughness has, understandably enough, replaced to a large extent a literature of beauty and rapture. Indeed, in the grim, desperate struggle for civilization's survival many people have been tempted to forget that the justification for that struggle is what civilization at its best can be.

If *Dance to the Piper* flames like a beacon in the midst of the present's darkness, it is because without being arty Miss de Mille dares to speak as an artist whose regard for what the arts must mean remains glowing and unshaken. Hers is a success story—with a difference.

In it Miss de Mille, instead of repeating the familiar rags-to-riches formula, recounts the adventures of a determined young woman who, in spite of parental objections and long, lean years of despair, rose from riches to justified recognition and triumph in *Rodeo* and *Oklahoma!* Her life history is a fabulous tale. It is the stirring and touching record of how a girl realized her dream when she escaped from the blighting conformity of being a lady. By the sheer granite of her character and the urgency of her own talents she became a good dancer in her own right, one of the foremost choreographers of our age, and certainly one of the best writers about her fellow dancers, dancing, and art in general our times have produced.

• Miss de Mille is almost unfairly endowed. Anyone who can dance or direct a ballet as well as she can ought not to be able to write as well as she does. Her gift for re-creating a scene is no less astonishing than her genius for capturing the essence of a personality. No one has painted a more vivid picture of Hollywood's early days. No one has so caught the smell and feel of such ballet schools as Kosloff's in Hollywood or Marie Rambert's in London. No one has more graphically described the tortures of barnstorming with a ballet troupe or the horrors and humiliations which can be suffered during the course of an out-of-town tryout of a Broadway musical. No one has ever told with more breathless suspense harrowing yarns which climb to happy endings.

Every personality she deals with—whether it is her father William de Mille, her Uncle Cecil, her indomitable mother (Anna George), Elinor Glyn, Geraldine Farrar, Douglass Montgomery, Pavlova, Isadora Duncan, Ruth St. Denis, John Martin, C. B. Cochran, Gertrude Lawrence, Antony Tudor, Tamara Toumanova, Hugh Laing, Adolph Bolm, Louis Horst, Martha Graham, Richard Rodgers, or Oscar Hammerstein 2nd—comes through as alive as if drawn by a skilful novelist who also happens to be an admirable portrait painter.

Miss de Mille's words and sentences dance. They have the vitality of her own ballets and are as original. They caper and race to their points with incredible energy and grace. Their groupings create unforgettable images. Yet burningly human, utterly candid, and studded with memorable sketches as *Dance to the Piper* is, it also benefits by the strength and clarity of Miss de Mille's exposition of the principles and purposes of all kinds of dancing.

As a theorist, Miss de Mille has the same lucidity and perception which distinguished the late André Levinson as a critic of the dance. She explains technical terms so that anyone can understand them, and writes of the final mysteries of a highly special profession in phrases that are at once simple and universal. The only book on the same subject that I can think of comparable to hers is Isadora Duncan's *My Life*. But where Isadora's autobiography, extraordinary as it was, suffered because its emphasis was more on her life than on her art and excluded from its pages those essays ultimately published in another volume called *The Art of the Dance,* Miss de Mille's personal history is as illuminating about her work as it is about her living.

Her book, though enthusiastically reviewed and a deserved best seller, has not in my opinion been praised as yet in the high terms it merits. More than insisting it is one of the most rewarding and absorbing books that I have read in several years, I would place it without hesitation among such notable volumes of theatrical reminiscences as Colley Cibber's *Apology,* the *Memoirs* of Gozzi and Goldoni, Stanislavsky's *My Life in Art*, Joseph Jefferson's *Autobiography,* Otis Skinner's *Footlights and Spotlights,* and Isadora Duncan's *My Life*. It, too, has the stuffs of greatness in it.

One of the troubles of the contemporary theatre is that so few of its people bring to their work that final, indestructible fanaticism, that unashamed yet very simple exaltation of the high priestess which Miss de Mille brings to dancing. Dancing to her is not a profession. It is a religion. When describing the words of advice and encouragement Martha Graham has given to others, Miss de Mille says, "One stood abashed, and listened. . . . There was the seal of her life upon them." The seal of Miss de Mille's life is upon every page and paragraph of *Dance to the Piper*.

March 15, 1952

Headmaster to the Universe

THE INCREDIBLE *Bernard Shaw*
and why, on the basis of his mind, spirit,
personality, and works, the world has
had to agree with his own high estimate
of himself.

Professional Man of Genius

O F COURSE, *Pygmalion* had a preface—even on the
screen. Otherwise it would not have been Shaw's. There
was the Old Gentleman himself, reading it as only the world's
best actor could. There he was, looking like that most unlikely
of mortals, a prophet with a sense of humor. There he was,
exuding the charm which is held to be Irish and was known to
be his. As usual, he was smiling his way through immodesties
and overstatements calculated to win attention and laughter.
No less characteristically, he was distributing insults as if they
were cookies, and persuading people to gobble them up as such.

And what was he saying in his role of self-appointed head-
master to the universe? "You will have to make up your mind
that you will lose me presently, and then heaven only knows
what will become of America. I have to educate all the nations.
I have to educate England. Several Continental nations require
a little educating, but America most of all. And I shall die before I have educated America properly, but I am making a
beginning."

All this was in 1938, a short-long twelve years ago, when
Shaw was a mere stripling of eighty-two. Now we have lost

him, and for many of us there is a kind of emptiness in the world. How the citizens of Rhodes felt when an earthquake toppled over the Colossus in their harbor, we do not know. We do know, however, the incredulity with which we face a universe without Shaw. In spite of increasing signs of his fatigue and warnings that he, too, must die, we had come to take his being here for granted. He was so palpably a natural phenomenon that we are bound to feel just now as if Niagara had dried up or Old Faithful had ceased to erupt.

When Mr. Roosevelt died, there were American teen-agers who, never having known any other President, could not imagine one. There are plenty of grandparents the globe over who, since their teens, have no memory of the literary scene when Shaw was not among the most towering of its landmarks. Longevity was one of his preachings which he practised. He practised it not only by keeping dazzlingly alive himself but by making this planet a far livelier—and different—place during those sixty years in which he functioned superbly as the challenger of every orthodoxy and the embodiment of his own Superman.

No one under seventy can pretend to have experienced the full detonating impact of Shaw when first he released the armory of his audacities against Victorianism in its every form. Those septuagenarians find it difficult even now to describe the heady delight and happy amazement with which they read him in their youth. They followed him gladly, not quite understanding or daring to understand, but with the joy of the emancipated. Although we, their children, got there later, there were plenty of wonders left and countless surprises.

We, too, knew the excitement of having him snatch the

bandages from our eyes and lead us out of the shadows into a realm of sunlight. He pricked our consciences, routed our smugness, jostled us into thoughts undreamed of. He gave us a new boldness, and an unbelievable illusion of freedom, all the while that he was providing us with pleasures fresh and to this day unequaled.

Since nothing is deader than an idea or a cause which no longer needs to be fought for, younger people encountering Shaw at present are bound to find some of his audacities tame and some of his arguments superfluous. They cannot be expected to know how much of what they assume has become accepted only because his fighting helped to make it so. Take the "New Woman" he so ardently championed. Certainly she has lost her youth and grown into a very, very old lady. But they fool themselves, these young people (in the manner of their elders), if they think they have caught up with Shaw. To the end he remained almost as far ahead of them as he was of their grandparents. The likelihood is that their great-great-grandchildren will follow his circuitous trail, panting and out-distanced.

In *Sixteen Self Sketches* Shaw's explanation of why he had never written a complete autobiography was that "things have not happened to me: on the contrary it is I who have happened to them." This was a statement, however unshrinking, of a truth from which no one can shrink. Shaw was not only a genius; he was an event. Someone likened him to a centipede with a foot in every cause. The range of his curiosities was so prodigious that the sun never set on his interests. From economics to religion, from government to painting, from history to music, drama to medicine, vivisection to literature, phonetics to Communism, the causes of war to the difficulties of peace, or yesterday's news to creative evolution, his mind leapt untiringly and with an athlete's prowess.

It was an extraordinary mind put to extraordinary uses. No one can read a page of Shaw's prefaces, his journalism, his letters, or his better plays without feeling its lunge, its force, magnificence, sparkle, and originality. It was an intellect giant-sized yet agile. In the field of letters only Voltaire's has been comparable with it in its mixture of lightness and vigor. It worked overtime and hummed like a dynamo.

It was an ebullient mind as sudden in its contradictions as it was constant in its brilliance. If it borrowed freely and unashamedly the coinage of other men's thinking, it nonetheless managed to melt down what it had appropriated and remint it into a currency glitteringly golden and unmistakably Shavian. Its lacks were plain enough, but its virtues were plainer still. It spoke for a man who had the courage to say what he felt instead of what he ought to have felt, and who possessed to a supreme degree a genius for illumination, stimulation, revelation, and provocation.

No subject daunted Shaw, and few were touched upon by him without at least having been made the more interesting. Was his Caesar in his apostrophe to the Sphinx convinced, without ever giving her a chance to speak, that he had read her riddle? Shaw himself was always ventriloquizing for the Sphinx, expecting her to be as quiet as a dream-wife while he spewed forth answers to all the problems known to men and gods. The fact that he was childless no more deterred him from pontificating (hilariously and quite sensibly) as the final authority on parenthood than the fact that he was a Socialist prevented him from marrying a millionairess and emitting angry cries of outrage when, as a millionaire himself, his taxes were mercilessly increased by a Labor Government.

Any Shavian can point out the inconsistencies in Shaw, and a lot of dullards as well as bright people have. But the Ph.D.'s in economics or government who will haunt his ghost in the years to come, sniffing and tracking down his deviations from himself, will always present the sorry picture of Lilliputians trying to take the measurements of a Brobdingnagian. Although they may, as the Bardolaters do, buy Bendixes at the expense of the man who is involuntarily their prey, they will only prove their own stature by trying to reduce his.

Even a literate student in a School of Education must be aware that Shaw is as apt to disagree with himself as he is to disagree with everyone else. Everyone knows that Henry George changed Shaw's life. Everyone knows that William Archer came across him in the British Museum (Shaw's university) with Marx's *Das Kapital* on one side of his desk and Wagner's score for the Nibelungen Ring on the other. And everyone who is not a citizen of Dogpatch must also know that Shaw, throughout his many teetotaling years, swerved like a drunken driver in his allegiances. By his own proud admission he was a crow who had followed many ploughs.

He was an Irishman who preferred England. He was a Fabian who became a capitalist. He was a defender of the people, indeed a soapbox orator, whose questionable gods at one time were Napoleon and Caesar. He was a champion of the downtrodden who flirted, briefly and dangerously, with the dictator-principle in terms of Mussolini, Hitler, and Stalin.

As Bartlett will remind those who have never read his essay on *Self-Reliance*, Emerson held a foolish consistency to be the hobgoblin of little minds, adored by little statesmen and philosophers and divines. Not even the fools who parade this world as wise men have accused Shaw of having a little mind. The dimensions of his mind can in a way be measured by its inconsistencies and perversities.

"It is an instinct with me," he once boasted, "to attack every idea which has been full grown for ten years, especially if it claims to be the foundation of all human society." This explains why his thinking wavered over the decades. This is why his opinions were subject to change without notice and beyond anticipation. His variability was a part of his irreplaceable value. His surprises were unceasing. What mattered most in Shaw was not what he thought but that he made others think.

In the essay already referred to, Emerson, who included among his gifts a talent for freshening the wilted lettuce of bromides, observed that to be great is to be misunderstood. No great man has, I will wager, embarked upon such a far-flung, deliberate, and successful conspiracy to be misunderstood as Shaw. To most of the pygmies (meaning you and me) who are not only well-mannered enough but sufficiently realistic to realize how pint-sized are whatever talents they may possess, Shaw has seemed a titanic egotist.

Take, for example, his assertion, "I should have been a clerk still if I had not broken loose in defiance of all prudence and become a professional man of genius—a resource not open to every clerk." Or his famous explosion, "With the exception of Homer, there is no eminent writer, not even Sir Walter Scott, whom I can despise so entirely as I despise Shakespeare when I measure my mind against his." Or his claim, "I know a great deal more about economics and politics than Jesus did and can do things he could not do."

These were utterances of which no finishing-school graduate

would have been guilty. Although they were shockers, planned with gleeful care, they were not meant to be blasphemous or even self-doting. On the subject of Jesus, about whom he has written beautifully, Shaw's only purpose was to point out the facts of economic and political change over the centuries.

So far as Shakespeare was concerned, he was (from his deep love and profound understanding of Shakespeare's merits) merely trying to make "a fellow creature" out of the Bard who had been "a divinity" and "a bore." He was doing this even while waging his usual warfare against Henry Irving and for "the drama of ideas" Ibsen had inaugurated. When it comes to Shaw's reference to himself as "a professional man of genius," he would have been a liar had he described himself in any other terms.

By temperament and habit Shaw was an honest man. The truth as he saw it, which was the truth as very few others had seen it or could bear to face or state it, always mattered more to him than such manners as the world expected. If, as he put it, he could not respond to the "demand for mock-modesty," neither was he ever guilty of mock-conceit. No one capable of writing and thinking as Shaw did could have failed to realize that when he wrote he was outwriting and outthinking other men.

Said he in 1944, "When I contemplate what I know and have done (not that I ever do) I have a high opinion of myself. When I contemplate what I don't know and cannot do (which I am often forced to do) I feel as a worm might if it knew how big the world is." He was equally candid when, in a passage dashed off nearly a half-century earlier, he wrote, "I am ashamed neither of my work nor of the way it is done. I like explaining its merits to the huge majority who don't know good work from bad. It does them good; and it does me good, curing me of nervousness, laziness, and snobbishness. . . . I leave the delicacies of retirement to those who are gentlemen first and literary workmen afterwards. The cart and trumpet for me."

Shaw never ceased being one of G.B.S.'s favorite subjects, and he made him a favorite subject throughout the world. No one has ever written about him so well as he has, and no one ever will. He was his own advance man to his own circus; his Dexter Fellowes to what beyond question was the Greatest Show on Earth.

As he phrased it, "Half my time is spent in telling people what a clever man I am. It is no use merely doing clever things in England. The English do not know what to think until they are coached, laboriously and insistently for years, in the proper and becoming opinion. For ten years past, with an unprecedented pertinacity and obstination, I have been dinning into the public head that I am an extraordinarily witty, brilliant, and clever man. That is now part of the public opinion of England and no power in heaven or on earth will ever change it. I may dodder and dote; I may potboil and platitudinize; I may become the butt and chopping block of all the bright, original spirits of the rising generation; but my reputation shall not suffer: it is built up fast and solid, like Shakespeare's, on an impregnable basis of dogmatic reiteration." This was 'way back in 1898 and must be hailed as one of Shaw's more accurate prophecies.

Plato got along very nicely by contenting himself with being Plato. But Shaw was a modern Plato who could not resist also being Puck and Pantaloon. When it comes to clowning, Grock and the Fratellinis were amateurs compared with him.

He could be downright silly. The gags he got off for the benefit of the wire services were often feeble, sometimes in questionable taste, and never dignified. If Shaw dispensed with
dignity, however, it was not only because it was alien to his
nature but because he did not need it. He had something far
rarer and finer to offer. He had grandeur.

His wit delighted the public but misled it. Conventional
people were confused by a man who said grave things gaily.
Their belief was that men who are to be taken seriously must
be dreary sobersides incapable of smiling. They found it easier
to pigeonhole him as a humorist when he pleased them and
as a buffoon when he shocked them. Shaw was well aware of
the dangers he invited by laughing. "I have got the tragedian
and I have got the clown in me," he once confessed, "and the
clown trips me up in the most dreadful way." He explained
this by saying that, like his father before him, he was in the
grip of a humorous sense of anticlimax.

As a prophet, an economist, propagandist, and social reformer, Shaw realized that his inconsistencies no less than his
wit blurred the effects he had hoped to achieve. The world
has been guilty of the sorry, if understandable, error of mistaking the paradoxes of G.B.S. for his purpose. Far more important than the polemicist, however, was the artist. The specific causes for which he fought have been or may be forgotten,
but the artist will always be remembered and treasured. Eric
Bentley once contended that the final paradox of Shaw's paradoxical career was that "by not saving the world [he] saved
his dramas as art and, therefore, as teaching."

Like Molière's doctor, Shaw was an artist in spite of himself.
He was the best, the sprightliest, the most deathless critic ever
to have reviewed plays. He was no less lively on the subjects

of painting and music. As *Pen Portraits and Reviews* makes blindingly clear, he was a journalist with Promethean powers of firing a reader's interest. Perhaps the final proofs of an instinctive writer's gifts are his letters. Shaw's letters and post-cards are miracles of invention, perception, gaiety, and fluency. We already have many samples of his superiority as a corre-spondent. We shall have more. Indeed, one of the greatest and most fascinating literary adventures the future will know is bound to be those many, many volumes of Shaw's letters which will some day be published, even as the Walpole and the Bos-well papers are now being issued.

Certainly *The Intelligent Woman's Guide to Socialism and Capitalism*, printed when Shaw was seventy-two, is one of the finest examples of expository writing on the subject of politics and economics known to any library. Then, of course, there are the plays—and the prefaces. Some of the plays are trifles. Others are dated. No one can say with any certainty which ones will speak most directly to unborn generations. But I, at least, would have only pity for a world which could not be touched by *Candida*, melted by *Androcles and the Lion*, amused by *Man and Superman* (including its scintillating interlude in Hell), quickened by *Caesar and Cleopatra*, and stirred by *Saint Joan*. Better than Shakespeare Shaw may not have been. Differ-ent he palpably was. Yet that his was the most fecund genius to have turned to the theatre since Shakespeare's time seems safe from challenge.

Shaw explained that he wrote prefaces, as Dryden did, "be-cause I *can*." I do not mean to subtract from the enrichment Dryden made to English prose when he was in a prefatory mood. I must insist, however, that Shaw's prefaces are in a class of their own. They are sizable additions to the gaiety of nations and the joys of reading. Prolix they may be. If they tire, however, it is only because in them Shaw gives us no rest from his own untiring brilliance.

"Effectiveness of assertion," he contended, "is the alpha and omega of style. He who has nothing to assert has no style and can have none." Shaw never lacked something to say and always said it with incredible vitality and apparently without effort. His sentences, as Winston Churchill (himself no mean stylist) observed, are colored with "a debating tinge."

The two vital qualities Shaw demanded of literature were "light and heat." Both of these his writing possessed to an unmatched degree. He did not believe, as many now seem to, that a great writer uses his skill to conceal his meaning. Although he did not object to writing for profit, he seldom wrote without a purpose. He had only contempt for "art for art's sake." However gay his words or bold his overstatements, Shaw's intentions were apt to be serious. He may have been the born mountebank he described himself as being, but he was also a puritan.

He was an author who, as a boy, had been brought up in a musical household. This training was not wasted on him. His prose has the dancing lightness and the shining precision of Mozart. It is also capable of deeper Wagnerian sonorities. Hazlitt described wit as "the eloquence of indifference." Shaw, however, was witty not because he did not care but because he did. He could also rise to passages of great melodic beauty. His plays are studded with speeches quivering with a prophet's fervor and with sentences which literally sing themselves. Although not written in verse, they make most contemporary dramatic speeches written as poetry seem like the most meager and muffled of prose.

· 69 ·

In spite of the multiplicity of his interests and his talents, the often ignored source of Shaw's greatness lay in the dimensions of his spirit. As surely as there was nothing little about his thinking, there was nothing little about his feeling. He never waged war on individuals. He waged war on the ideas for which they stood. His gift for forgiveness was even greater than his need at times to be forgiven. He was essentially good, kindly, clean, and gentle. His spiritual largeness explains why he, the supposed clown and acknowledged wit, was able to understand the dilemmas of such a man of action as Caesar, and to write in *Androcles and the Lion* and *Saint Joan* the two most beautiful religious plays to have come out of the modern theatre.

Although Shaw, the iconoclast, saw through men and institutions, he never lost his hope for what men might become if only they resolved to live up to their potentialities and outgrow their present limitations. The Life-Force, about which he wrote, was a potent factor in his own living. His plea was for progress. He loathed the shirkers, the loafers, the talent-squanderers, and time-wasters who deny themselves "the true joy in life" by not being used for a purpose they recognize "as a mighty one." The demands he made on himself were as unrelenting as those he made on others. Yes, and on God, too.

It is something to have lived on this planet as the contemporary of such a titan as George Bernard Shaw. Although he was mortal enough to die, we have not lost him. Of him it can be truly said, as he said of William Morris, "You can lose a man like that by your own death, but not by his."

November 18, 1950

*A LADY who was for burning, and for
sainthood too, as Shaw points out the
meaning of her martyrdom in* Saint
Joan.

The Prophet and the Maid

STATEMENTS beyond challenge are as rare as virtue un-
tested. In spite of this, it would seem safe to say that *Saint
Joan* * is not only Shaw's greatest play but one of the greatest
plays to have come out of the modern theatre. Yet as I write
these words I realize their rashness. I recall how even *Hamlet*,
a tragedy the world has been dull enough to accept as a masterpiece, was once dismissed by T. S. Eliot as being "most certainly an artistic failure."

It is this same Olympian Mr. Eliot, however, who at this
moment gives me courage. In his recent *Poetry and Drama*
he has admitted that his *Murder in the Cathedral* may have
been written "slightly under the influence of *Saint Joan.*" Such
a statement from such a source, though not expressed in the
ordinary terms of praise, is no doubt meant to be taken as praise
from Sir Hubert. I know it makes me feel the safer from attack

* *Saint Joan,* by Bernard Shaw. Directed by Margaret Webster. Settings
by Richard Harrison Senie. Costumes by Elinor Robbins. Music by Lehman
Engel. Produced by the Theatre Guild under the supervision of Theresa
Helburn and Lawrence Langner. With a cast including Uta Hagen, John
Buckmaster, Andrew Cruickshank, Alexander Scourby, Robert Pastene,
Frederic Worlock, Frederic Warriner, Paul Ballantyne, Frederick Rolf,
John Straub, Kendall Clark, Preston Hanson, etc. At the Cort Theatre.
Opened October 4, 1951.

when I assert that most people (notice I say "most") have a special and rightful admiration for Shaw's drama about the Maid who heard voices.

Saint Joan may not have been Shaw's own favorite among his works. In her *Thirty Years with G.B.S.* Blanche Patch reports it was not. She reveals that in Frank Harris's copy of *Heartbreak House* Shaw wrote, "Rightly spotted by the infallible eye of Frank Harris as My Best Play." Nonetheless, to the majority of Shavians, regardless of how high is their esteem for other plays by him, *Saint Joan* is his masterpiece.

Shaw was sixty-seven when he finished it in 1923, and Joan had been made a saint only three years before. Her posthumous fate had not been without its ironies. As Shaw reminds us, she had been burned for heresy, witchcraft, and sorcery in 1431; rehabilitated after a fashion in 1456; designated venerable in 1904; declared Blessed in 1908; and finally canonized in 1920.

There was everything about Joan as a subject to interest Shaw, and everything about her to release his mightiest gifts once his interest had been won. Yet apparently he resisted Joan as a theme and would have continued to do so had not Charlotte Shaw employed strategy to get her husband started on a play she wanted him to write. Being a good wife, in other words a woman blessed with Maggie Shand's knowledge, she did not argue with Shaw or let him feel that she was influencing him. Instead, she left books about the Maid and her trial around the house in places where he was certain to see them, pick them up, and read them in his moments of idleness. He fell for the bait and, once having fallen, became absorbed in Joan.

When *Saint Joan* first appeared there were many even among the most stalwart of Shaw's followers who were surprised by the reverence of the play which the notoriously irreverent G.B.S. had written. They had long since admitted his brilliance. They had recognized his audacity. They had prized his originality and laughed at his jokes. But they had grown so accustomed to identifying him as a professional iconoclast and jester that they had lost sight of his seriousness. Remembering his wit, they had forgotten his eloquence. They had closed their eyes to the fact that his spirit was as sizable as his mind. Above all, they had failed to recall, or, worse still, misunderstood, *Androcles and the Lion* and the noble simplicity of the scene in which the Roman soldier asks the Christian woman who is about to face martyrdom in the arena, "What is God?" and she answers, "When we know that, Captain, we shall be gods ourselves."

A man who in Shaw's manner could refuse his Government's offer of the Order of Merit by saying he had already conferred it upon himself was bound to be suspected by the humorless of immodesty. When it came to *Saint Joan,* however, he was far more modest than he had any right or cause to be. Hesketh Pearson reports that Shaw said to Sybil Thorndike, the first actress to play the part in England, "I have told the story exactly as it happened. It is the easiest play I have ever had to write. All I've done is to put down the facts, to arrange Joan for the stage. The trial scene is merely a report of the actual trial. I have used Joan's very words: thus she spoke, thus she behaved."

Count this among the least reliable of Shavian utterances. In *Saint Joan* Shaw matters at every turn and with the turn of almost every phrase. What makes the play magnificent is not that he retells the familiar story but that this story comes to life in a new and memorable way as the issues involved and the problems raised by Joan provoke his eloquence, appeal to his mysticism, stir his imagination, and ignite his thinking.

Though a Protestant himself, Shaw refuses to use Joan's trial and burning as a means of attacking the Catholic Church. With all the fairness of his incredibly fair mind he insists she was given a very careful and conscientious trial by men who were anxious to save her.

To understand her fate, he points out, one must understand not only her character and claims but the mind and beliefs of the Middle Ages. Joan's paradox, he maintains, was that though a professed and most pious Catholic she was in fact one of the first Protestant martyrs. In a feudal period when nobles were jealous of their prerogatives, she imperiled these prerogatives by being an early exponent of nationalism and championing the powers of her king. That a country girl in her teens presumed to tell military leaders what they should do was bound to antagonize the Brass Hats to whom she gave orders. Moreover, she was an individualist who invited religious disfavor by claiming that she could speak directly to God through her visions and voices without the intercession of the Church.

Beyond and above these causes for Joan's unpopularity with her contemporaries there were, as Shaw demonstrates, other and more disconcerting reasons for her undoing. Because she was exceptional her contemporaries could not tolerate her, and because she was their moral superior they burned her. Indeed, the point of Shaw's play is summarized by two ageless questions asked in the Epilogue. The first is Cauchon's "Must then a Christ perish in torment in every age to save those that have no imagination?" The second is Joan's "O God that madest this beautiful earth, when will it be ready to receive Thy saints? How long, O Lord, how long?"

The dimensions of the tragedy (the poetry of its prose, the unfettering simplicity of its construction, its tenderness, its intellectual power, indeed its grandeur) are unmistakable throughout. No scene in the modern theatre is more touching as an affirmation of faith than the one by the banks of the Loire when the wind changes. None is more charged with the electricity of ideas than the discussion by Cauchon, Warwick, and De Stogumber of the religious and political problems raised by the Maid. No on-stage trial is more stirring than Joan's and no single speech mightier in its language than the one addressed to the court by the Inquisitor. As for the Epilogue, it is hard to see why it was subject to furious attacks when the play was originally produced. It is the needed summary of what has gone before and is essential to our understanding both of Shaw's meaning and of Joan's posthumous fate and ultimate canonization.

Any production of *Saint Joan* is bound to be as dependent upon the actress playing Joan as *Hamlet* is upon the actor who plays the Prince. The present production, as directed by Margaret Webster, has its genuine merits. It moves swiftly. It is set and costumed in an acceptable enough style. And in Kendall Clark's sensitive Brother Martin, the fire of Robert Pastene's Dunois, the sinister brilliance of Andrew Cruickshank's Warwick, and the complete and hilarious excellence of John Buckmaster's Dauphin, it achieves distinction. Even so something is lacking. The full fervor of the text is not communicated. In such a scene, for example, as the lovely one by the Loire the mere mechanics of the production fail to create the sense of the miraculous. Then, too, the Inquisitor's great plea for tolerance (a plea never more needed than today) is tamely read by Frederick Rolf. But, to my way of thinking, the production's major disappointment comes in Uta Hagen's Joan.

Although Miss Hagen has on many occasions demonstrated how fine a performer she is, Joan eludes her. She has her good scenes, reads intelligently, and is properly earthy and unsentimental. At her best, however, she is no more than competent, and at her worst plainly inadequate. The final requisite for Joan is that inner radiance which is in the text and which flamed in Katharine Cornell's performance. This is missing, and the absence of this simple, shimmering spirituality is a major loss.

Several actresses have played Joan, and many more will. But the Joan of all Joans I should like to have heard—and seen— was the one Margaret Webster once told me was the best she ever saw. It was Bernard Shaw himself; Shaw when he read the part to Sybil Thorndike's company in which Miss Webster was an understudy. Apparently as one listened to his marvelously flexible and musical voice, his beard and age, his sex and dress were all forgotten, and the spirit of the real Joan, his Joan, came magically to life.

Doubtless Shaw read his Joan as well as he had written her because both he and she, by his own insistence, were geniuses. A genius, says he in his superb preface to the play, "is a person who, seeing farther and probing deeper than other people, has a different set of ethical values from theirs, and has energy enough to give effect to this extra vision and its valuations in whatever manner best suits his or her specific talents." No wonder, therefore, the old Prophet understood the young Maid so well, or that from his understanding he was able to write a play the greatness of which cannot be obscured even in a production that fails to do justice to its splendors.

October 27, 1951

*A HEAVENLY evening in a Hell
where ideas are the plot, wit is the lighting, eloquence the scenery, and four fine
actors do justice to a memorable script.*

What—Shaw Again?

YES, BECAUSE he makes it inescapable. Yes, because his
deathless voice has once again brought our so-called living
theatre to life. Yes, because for the second time in a season up
to now cursed and largely overrun by the efforts of pygmies
he has stood out like a colossus, an intellect among the thought-
less, a genius among hacks, and a seer among the blind.

It is the *Don Juan in Hell* * scene from *Man and Superman*,
as read by Charles Laughton, Charles Boyer, Cedric Hardwicke, and Agnes Moorehead, which leaves me with no other
inclination or choice than to write about Shaw once more. For
some time now audiences in city after city up and down the
United States (and England, too) have had the opportunity
to enjoy this seldom performed interlude that Shaw wrote fifty
years ago. Now, at last, an underprivileged New York has been
permitted to respond to its excitements.

Nothing Broadway has had to offer since Laurence Olivier's
Oedipus has been more absorbing than this theatrically unor-

* *Don Juan in Hell*, by Bernard Shaw. Directed by Charles Laughton. The
First Drama Quartette presented by Paul Gregory. With Mr. Laughton,
Charles Boyer, Cedric Hardwicke, and Agnes Moorehead. At Carnegie Hall,
October 22, 1951. At Century Theatre, November 29–December 31, 1951.
At Plymouth Theatre, March 31–May 31, 1952.

thodox presentation of a play which is not a play in the ordinary sense. The performance is in the nature of a reading. Only a shallow forestage is used and it is backed by a black curtain. In front of this curtain are microphones and stools, and music stands to hold the bound copies of the text carried in by the actors. The three men are dressed in dinner jackets and Miss Moorehead wears an evening gown. Mr. Laughton briefly and charmingly tells the essentials of the Don Juan story and announces the cast. Thereafter he leads us into the script by letting us hear Shaw's stage direction. As far as the trappings of production go, that is all. But what an all and what an evening it proves to be!

If any members of Local 829 managed to squeeze into Carnegie Hall, they—and they alone—in a huge and rapt audience must have felt a certain discomfort. They may even have had a clearer understanding of Othello's feelings when he complained his occupation was gone. For Local 829 is the United Scenic Artists. And here was Shaw proving, as Shakespeare demonstrated long ago, how unnecessary scenery is when great language sets the stage.

Anyone can cite examples of the way in which Shakespeare relied on his pen to do the brushwork most contemporary playwrights assume will be done for them by scene designers with the aid of dependable electricians. In *Macbeth* the First Murderer's "The west yet glimmers with some streaks of day"; Horatio's "But look, the morn, in russet mantle clad,/ Walks o'er the dew of yon high eastward hill . . ."; and Lorenzo's "The moon shines bright. In such a night as this,/ When the sweet wind did gently kiss the trees/ And they did make no noise . . ." are familiar instances of the kind of verbal scenery Shakespeare supplied in play after play.

Shaw's employment of the language proves no less self-sufficient in this uncostumed and unset "reading" of *Don Juan in Hell.* Yet there is a striking difference. Shaw has no interest in conjuring images to evoke a physical setting. He makes fun of Dante for having described hell as a place of mud, frost, filth, fire, and venomous serpents. He is equally contemptuous of Milton for having introduced cannon and gunpowder as a means of expelling the Devil from heaven. Shaw's hell is visually nonexistent. In his own words "there is nothing; omnipresent nothing. No sky, no peaks, no light, no sound, no time nor space, utter void." There is only somewhere the faint throbbing buzz of a Mozartian strain and a pallor which "reveals a man in the void, an incorporeal but visible man, seated, absurdly enough, on nothing."

In the course of *Don Juan* Shaw pays tribute to the wonders of that slowly evolved bodily organ, the eye, which has permitted the living organism to "see where it was going and what was coming to help or threaten it." Even so his concern is with neither the eye nor the visible world. Instead, it is with the evolving mind's eye and its higher plane of vision which should enable us to see "the purpose of Life." He makes his hell a void so that he can fill it with ideas. His intellect sets the stage; his fervor and his wit light it. What absorbs his attention and ours is not a place but the plight of Man. It is Man's foolishness and his potentialities; what he has been, what he is, and what he must become if he is either to justify his existence or safeguard his survival.

There are those beyond counting who expect a play to have a plot. They want it at least to tell how Jack gets Jill or Jill Jack. The story of Ann Whitefield's pursuit and conquest of John Tanner is the narrative basis of *Man and Superman,* into the third act of which *Don Juan in Hell* is tucked as a detachable dream sequence. Being spirits, the characters in this interlude are no longer plotbound.

Having already lived their personal histories, the Devil, the Commander, Doña Ana, and Don Juan are free in hell to concentrate on a far larger, more universal story—the story of Mankind. This is the subject of their dialogue. To be more accurate, it is the theme of their "great debate." Although they do nothing except talk, such talk is in itself an exciting activity. The very thrust and fascination of their arguments create drama. Due to the mind at work, this battle of ideas is far more dramatic in its action than a thousand trumped-up plots.

Shaw's hell has nothing in common with the hell that fires the imagination of those who hit the sawdust trail. It is not even the satanic realm with which milder ministers are fond of threatening sinners. Instead, it is as unconventional an inferno as only Shaw could make it. He establishes it as a delightful retreat for seekers after happiness who intellectually and spiritually have not outgrown its pleasures. Its pleasures are such that it is visited frequently by those who are bored with heaven.

Shaw's heaven is no less exceptional. It is open only to those who have become the masters of reality. This sets it very much apart from earth, where mortals are reality's slaves. In this Shavian paradise what is done cannot be undone by repentance and spoken words cannot be unspoken by withdrawing them, any more than the truth can be annihilated by a general agreement to give it the lie.

One of Shaw's most typical and engaging paradoxes is that such a heaven attracts, of all people, Don Juan the libertine. Juan has tired of the license which won him earthly fame and come to see the emptiness of the diversions offered him in hell. His belief in Man is greater than the Devil's disbelief. The Devil may argue against heaven and Man with all the skill at Shaw's command, but it is to this heavenly refuge of realists that Don Juan is determined to go. And go he finally does, as the champion of the Life-Force, Creative Evolution, and the Superman.

Most readers and playgoers remember lines from Shaw's memorable preface to *Man and Superman,* from the play and the interlude, or from *The Revolutionist's Handbook,* which concludes the volume. None of Shaw's works bulges with more passages which refuse to be forgotten and cry to be quoted. His mind never had freer play than in *Don Juan in Hell.* His prowess as a debater was never more irrefutably established than in the discussion where the voices of Shaw and Anti-Shaw are heard, and each is given the benefit of all Shaw's eloquence, wit, and moral passion. Following such an argument may make hard demands on those unable to concentrate and antagonistic to thought. But in spite of G.B.S.'s confessed wordiness, listening, to anyone with half a mind, has seldom been easier or more rewarding.

One of the incredible aspects of *Don Juan in Hell* is that it remains utterly and urgently contemporary. The half-century which has passed since it was written has left it undated. Take, for example, the Devil's speech in the first part of the evening when he appears to have the better of the debate. Don Juan has claimed that Man's hope lies in his brain. "And is Man any the less destroying himself for all this boasted brain of his?" asks the Devil. "Have you walked up and down upon the earth lately? I have; and I have examined Man's wonderful inventions. And I tell you that in the arts of life man invents nothing; but in the arts of death he outdoes Nature herself, and produces by chemistry and machinery all the slaughter of plague, pestilence, and famine. The peasant I tempt today eats and drinks what was eaten and drunk by the peasants of ten thousand years ago; and the house he lives in has not altered as much in a thousand centuries as the fashion of a lady's bonnet in a score of weeks. But when he goes out to slay, he carries a marvel of mechanism that lets loose at the touch of his finger all the hidden molecular energies, and leaves the javelin, the arrow, the blowpipe of his fathers far behind. In the arts of peace Man is a bungler."

Towards the end of the present "reading," divided as it is into two parts so as to ease the strain of taut listening, Don Juan speaks not only for himself but for Shaw. "I tell you," he insists, "that as long as I can conceive something better than myself I cannot be easy unless I am striving to bring it into existence or clearing the way for it. That is the law of my life. That is the working within me of Life's incessant aspiration to higher organization, wider, deeper, intenser self-consciousness, and clearer self-understanding. It was the supremacy of this purpose that reduced love for me to the mere pleasure of a moment, art for me to the mere schooling of my faculties, religion for me to a mere excuse for laziness, since it had set up a God who looked at the world and saw that it was good, against the instinct in me that looked through my eyes at the world and saw that it could be improved. I tell you that in the pursuit of my own pleasure, my own health, my own fortune, I have never known happiness."

Thus the Don Juan-Shaw—entirely uncynical. Thus Shaw, the philosophic man, with all his energies in revolt against the wrong or the merely adequate, and mobilized in a campaign for improvement. Thus Shaw, the militant reformer, the wrecker who destroys to rebuild, the firm believer in the "continual ascent of Man on the stepping stones of his dead selves to higher things." Thus Shaw with his conviction that Man's need and hope lie in evolving into a being better than he now is. Thus Shaw with his extension of the theory of the Superman which he derived from Nietzsche, who, though named in the original text, is for some strange reason left unmentioned in the present version.

The performance *Don Juan* is given is far more than a reading and in every respect worthy of Shaw's writing. Although it has an irresistible informality, it can claim a splendid dignity. Among its igniting qualities count the fact that it puts the imagination to stimulating work at the same time that it keeps the mind racing with delight. The members of the Quartette read from memory rather than from their texts. This is what makes "reading" so inadequate a word as a description of the presentation. A reading can be a painful affair, as everyone must recall with a shiver who sat through *Macbeth* as Dr. Edith Sitwell and her co-vocalists elegantly murdered both Shakespeare and the tragedy. The reading of *Don Juan* is as life-giving as the other was life-taking.

Charles Laughton has directed his associates so that they play beautifully and generously together. Perhaps it would be more accurate to say he has conducted the performance, treating the script as both the intellectual and vocal score it is. He and his actors have given their whole minds to Shaw's words, and by having done so they make it the easier for us to give our whole minds too.

Long and triumphant experience as a public reader has made Mr. Laughton a virtuoso of platform appearances. He is entirely at home in an enterprise of this kind. His moon-round face is quick to register and project every needed nuance of expression. His voice is equally flexible. It is a fine, rich, varied instrument, fortified by the most precise diction. His Satan is a doubly dangerous fellow for being so ingratiating in the ingenuity, the perversity, and the persuasiveness with which he states his diabolical arguments.

Charles Boyer is no less fine. Charming as he is, he turns his back resolutely on the kind of Boyer charm that in movie after movie transformed dowagers into bobby-soxers. From the moment he first speaks his Don Juan is a man no longer interested in his earthly pursuits. He is tired of the frivolities of the hell in which he finds himself, and inspired with a purpose. He is high-spirited, yet behind his smile and his gift for gaiety there is a glowing zeal which is the foundation of his faith. His French accent may occasionally create some difficulties, but these are few and unimportant. Well as he reads throughout (using "reads" in the ordinary theatrical sense of understanding and communicating an author's meaning), he rises to stirring heights of prophetic eloquence when he releases and illumines the magnificent speeches in which the Shavian credo of affirmation is ultimately stated.

Though Cedric Hardwicke, as the Commander, and Agnes Moorehead, as Doña Ana, have the lesser parts, they contribute richly to the evening. Mr. Hardwicke suggests to the full the arrogance of the military type and speaks, as always, with his mind in full command of his tongue. Miss Moorehead is highly pictorial, possessing visually something of the quality of Sargent's Madame X. She makes the most of the text's least interesting part. May I add, however, that the writing which is least interesting in *Don Juan in Hell* is a hundred times more interesting than that to be found in most recent plays.

Surely, no dramatic critic has performed for the theatre a finer service than A. B. Walkley's when he urged Shaw to write a drama about Don Juan. No less surely, few contemporary actors have performed a greater service to Shaw, the theatre, and all of us than this Quartette of excellent actors by letting us see and hear *Don Juan in Hell*.

November 10, 1951

Beyond Prose

CLEOPATRA, first the kitten, then passion's slave, as seen in two plays as different as only an emotionalist who ate roast beef and a rational vegetarian could make them.

ਤਰਤਰਤਰਤਰਤਰਤਰਤਰਤਰਤਰਤਰਤਰਤਰਤਰਤਰਤਰਤਰਤਰ

A Queen's Story

THE SUGGESTION was Roger Furse's. Advanced as a joke, it has proved an inspiration. Laurence Olivier and Vivien Leigh were anxious to find a play which they could present in London in time for the Festival of Britain. But they were both tired after a term in Hollywood and their cupboard of ideas was bare. "What about *Caesar and Cleopatra?**" someone asked. Remembering the indifferent film version in which she had appeared, Miss Leigh was against it. No one can blame her. It was then that Roger Furse, the designer, spoke up. "Let's do the two Cleopatras," he said smilingly, "the Shaw and the Shakespeare. We could save money with a single billing." Although the Oliviers dismissed the notion as impractical and thought Mr. Furse was being funny, fortunately for all of us, as the days passed and they were still without plans,

* *Caesar and Cleopatra*, by Bernard Shaw, and *Antony and Cleopatra*, by William Shakespeare, acted on alternate nights. Directed by Michael Benthall. Settings by Roger Furse. Costumes by Audrey Cruddas. Music by Herbert Menges. Presented by Gilbert Miller by arrangement with Laurence Olivier Productions, Ltd. With a cast including Laurence Olivier, Vivien Leigh, Robert Helpmann, Wilfrid Hyde White, Harry Andrews, Niall MacGinnis, Pat Nye, Harold Kasket, Dan Cunningham, etc. At the Ziegfeld Theatre, New York City. Opened December 19, 1951.

they came to take him seriously with results that have made stage history.

Only Plutarch, with his mastery of antithesis, could do justice to the dissimilarities separating *Caesar and Cleopatra* from *Antony and Cleopatra*. The two dramas are as unlike as Shaw and Shakespeare. The one is a comedy, the work of a rationalist; the other, a tragedy, the outpouring of an emotionalist. The first recognizes no passion except moral passion; the second has no morals in it and is all passion. The modern play is written in prose as eloquent as only Shaw could make it; the Elizabethan in poetry as glorious as Shakespeare alone, and at his most magnificent, could produce it.

Caesar and Cleopatra is concerned with the wise use of greatness and power, *Antony and Cleopatra* with their wanton squandering and abuse. The subject of the one is wisdom; of the other, lust. Julius Caesar is a conqueror in control of himself no less than of kingdoms; Mark Antony, a conqueror so conquered by his desires that he has kissed kingdoms away. Shaw, the puritan, feeling only revulsion at sexual infatuation when treated as a tragic theme, chose to present his Cleopatra as a young girl, unsure of herself, frightened at first, and sorely in need of the lessons in how to rule given her by the mighty Julius. Shakespeare, burningly aware of the pains and ecstasies, the ardors and costs of sexual infatuation, elected to present his Cleopatra as a mature woman, capricious and wayward and flaming with passion. Where the one Cleopatra is a kitten growing up to be a queen, the other is a tigress so much the slave of her emotions that she has almost forgotten her duties as a queen. The result of Shaw's approach is a play witty, wise, and absorbing; the result of Shakespeare's is a drama soaring, sublime in its beauties, and turbulent in its excitements.

Drastic as are the differences which separate them, *Caesar and Cleopatra* and *Antony and Cleopatra* do complement each other, and to a surprising degree. The differences do not keep them from fitting together as neatly as if they were instalments in a serial. No wonder the title by which they are known on Broadway is "Two on the Nile." Since for the first time they can be seen on successive nights as given by the same company, wise theatregoers will see them both and in their proper sequence. Furthermore, judgment should be withheld until both have been seen. Then, and then only, can the unexpected unity of the two plays be realized, the strategy of the performances understood, and the magnitude of the whole brave, dazzling undertaking appreciated.

The links uniting the plays do not stop with the obvious ones. There is more to the connection between them than the fact that they deal with earlier and later incidents in Cleopatra's life and hence have the continuity of episodes in a biography. Both are as involved with the sweep of Rome's imperial power on its highest levels as they are with individuals greatly placed. An unmistakable bridge is supplied, too, by Shaw. His Cleopatra has already met Mark Antony and is haunted by the memory of the "beautiful young man with strong round arms."

Moreover, Shaw's Julius promises to send her this same Antony as a replacement. He is an Antony described by Shaw at the conclusion of his play in Shakespearean terms; a "Roman from head to heel and Roman of the noblest; not old and ripe for the knife; not lean in the arms and cold in the heart; not hiding a bald head under his conqueror's laurels; not stooped with the weight of the world on his shoulders; but brisk and fresh, strong and young, hoping in the morning, fighting in the day, and reveling in the evening."

There are other points in common. The disasters courted by Shakespeare's Serpent of the Nile are the penalties she pays for not having mastered the lessons in clemency, wisdom, and large-heartedness which Shaw's conqueror tried to teach the girlish queen. Shaw's script serves, therefore, as an illuminating prologue to the tragedy which follows it. If the tragedy is by far the mightier play, finding Shakespeare greater than Shaw rather than Shaw "better than Shakespeare," this in no way subtracts from the originality and brilliance of Shaw's writing. He is the only modern dramatist I can think of who would stand up at all when presented on the same program with Shakespeare. In spite of fighting a losing battle, he stands up very well.

Among the points in his favor count the fact that in Enobarbus Shakespeare created without realizing it an admirable Shavian character. Although Shaw would never have permitted him to apostrophize the beauties of Cleopatra's barge in such shamelessly un-Fabian terms, Enobarbus is blessed with Shaw's own sanity. It is a sanity born not of disenchantment but of having the courage, so often mistaken for the perversity of wit, to see and describe things as they are.

The interest in the current joint bill lies, of course, not only in the two plays, which are available everywhere in print, but more especially in what is done to them in these Olivier productions. The Oliviers have come to occupy a unique and commanding position in the English-speaking theatre no less than on the screen. Their careers, important as well as glamorous, have been of so ascendant a kind that their mere names send expectations skyrocketing.

Stay-at-home Americans are far more familiar with Mr. Olivier's powers as a legitimate actor than with Miss Leigh's.

But all moviegoers who saw her in such pictures as *Gone with the Wind* and *A Streetcar Named Desire* have recognized her rare abilities. I regret to say I missed such of her London stage successes as *The Skin of Our Teeth* and *Streetcar*. I did, however, see her in *The Doctor's Dilemma* and realized then how much she had grown since she and Mr. Olivier brought their ill-fated *Romeo and Juliet* to New York eleven years ago.

As for Mr. Olivier, moviegoers still, and rightly, remember him with gratitude in *Wuthering Heights* and *Rebecca* and for his superb *Henry V*, that best of all good pictures, and his *Hamlet*, varied as it was in its merits. Certainly Americans, already acquainted with his work in *Private Lives*, *The Green Bay Tree*, and *No Time for Comedy*, became aware of his astonishing versatility when he appeared in New York with the Old Vic in such dissimilar parts as Hotspur, Justice Shallow, Puff, and Astrov. When they sat before his *Oedipus*, which was one of the modern theatre's most memorable and exciting performances, they were forced to admit that, more than being a remarkable actor, Mr. Olivier was a great one.

In the two *Cleopatras* the Oliviers face a stern challenge. They not only have to live up to their own reputations but to live down vivid recollections of Katharine Cornell and Godfrey Tearle in *Antony and Cleopatra* and of Lilli Palmer and Cedric Hardwicke in *Caesar and Cleopatra*.

It would be silly and churlish to pretend that these recent revivals, both of which were admirable, did not boast excellences sometimes unmatched in the current productions. Miss Palmer was bewitchingly impetuous and attractive as the kittenish Cleopatra; Mr. Hardwicke, a brilliant and persuasive Julius, far younger in appearance and more military in bearing than the tired conqueror Mr. Olivier has chosen to portray.

Miss Cornell was ravishing as the mature Cleopatra, and in her death scene achieved a tragic splendor and did a justice to the glories of the poetry Miss Leigh fails to equal. As the fallen Antony, Mr. Tearle succeeded even more completely than Mr. Olivier in being the embodiment of greatness wrecked and in suggesting a genius for command robbed of its self-command.

When it comes to the world-ranging political considerations in *Antony and Cleopatra,* which are so essential a part of the personal tragedies involved, these seemed to me more clearly and urgently stated in the Cornell-McClintic production than in the Olivier. As far as some of the secondary performances are concerned, I must confess that I found Douglass Watson's Eros heartbreaking and unforgettable where Lyndon Brook's is less than indifferent, and Harry Andrews's Enobarbus woefully inadequate compared to Kent Smith's wholly distinguished characterization which was as wise, touching, and commanding as the part requires. Although I admire Robert Helpmann's ability to turn successfully from such a lighthearted hedonist as Apollodorus in Shaw's play to Shakespeare's Octavius Caesar, I miss in his performance, tight-lipped, arrogant, and persuasive as it is, the cold, modern-dictator inhumanity and military appearance which Ralph Clanton brought to the part in the Cornell production.

These are among the reservations honesty demands. Like many reservations, however, including some yet to come, they are irrelevances so far as the stunning merits and compelling virtues of the Oliviers' offerings are concerned. I mention them not to be disagreeable but to be fair. I cite them because only when they are admitted can the true and exceptional attributes of the present productions be properly evaluated.

Lovely as Miss Cornell was as Shakespeare's mature queen,

she could not have alternated her with Shaw's kittenish Cleopatra. Excellent as Mr. Hardwicke was as Shaw's Julius, Shakespeare's Antony would have been beyond his range. Mr. Tearle, so right in that part, would have his troubles as Caesar, the benevolent dictator, if for no other reason than that his resemblance to F.D.R. would bring more delight to Republicans than to Shakespeareans or historians. As for Miss Palmer, richly endowed as she is, she has yet to prove that she is equal to the tragic grandeur to which the dying Cleopatra must rise.

Miss Leigh, as her Cleopatras make clear, is far more than a beautiful woman possessed of an electric personality. She is an actress capable of the infinite variety of the two Cleopatras. She can be the kitten to perfection, playing the earlier Shavian scenes with all the farcical lightness the text requires. Then, visibly, she can put girlhood behind her and grow into an adult and a monarch. If her young Cleopatra is unaware of her allure, it is because Miss Leigh is hoarding her passion for Shakespeare's queen, even as Mr. Olivier as Julius Caesar is saving his youth for Mark Antony. To a degree I would not have believed possible, Miss Leigh succeeds in matching the ever-changing moods and meeting the heavy demands of Shakespeare's heroine. In the course of the two evenings she demonstrates that she is able to be coy, frightened, impudent, cruel, lustful, imperious, comedic, and tragic in the most complete portrait of Cleopatra the theatre has known or is apt to know.

Mr. Olivier's Caesar and Antony are both distinguished. His Julius takes Shaw's script too literally and is older than he ought to be. When Caesar went to Egypt he was, after all, only in his early fifties. To Cleopatra, then sixteen, he unquestionably looked like the "old gentleman" referred to in the dialogue. Mr. Olivier, however, has made himself up so that he looks like an old gentleman even to those who are themselves in their early fifties. Although Shaw preferred to forget Caesarion, Caesar's son by Cleopatra, Caesarion would have been unknown to history had Caesar been as venerable and as tired as Mr. Olivier makes him. I, for one, can see no reason why as Julius Mr. Olivier should not carry himself more like a professional soldier, and save his slouch as a characterizing value for Antony. I also wish that, instead of subduing his voice as he does at times in both parts, Mr. Olivier would grant his Caesar and his Antony the benefit of its full resonance and strength.

But make no mistake about it. Mr. Olivier's performances are such as only a remarkable actor could give. He knows the mind and spirit of Shaw's conqueror. His Julius is as wise as his Antony is abandoned, as intellectual as the latter is physical, and both of them are men to whom authority comes naturally. Few can equal Mr. Olivier and none excel him when it comes to reading prose or poetry so that their ultimate beauty and meaning are revealed. He is a master not only of small details but of great scenes, and blessed with a gift for comedy no less marked than his gift for tragedy.

Some inadequate mention must be made of the sweep and intelligence of Michael Benthall's direction, of the serviceability of Roger Furse's settings, and the general excellence of the company the Oliviers have brought with them, with special reference to Wilfrid Hyde White as Britannus and Lepidus, Robert Helpmann as Apollodorus and Octavius, Niall MacGinnis's Rufio and Pompey, and Harold Kasket as Pothinus and Mardian.

What matters, what is exciting, what lends distinction to this season, and would to any other, is to have two such players as the Oliviers giving fine performances in two such notable plays.

January 12, 1952

*LEAR AND ELIA, or the strange way
in which Charles Lamb's gentle voice
makes itself heard above the old monarch's when on the heath the king must
outroar the storm.*

⹊⹊⹊⹊⹊⹊⹊⹊⹊⹊⹊⹊⹊⹊⹊⹊⹊⹊⹊⹊⹊⹊⹊⹊⹊⹊⹊⹊⹊⹊⹊⹊

Lear's Kingdom

THEY form an odd twosome, the mild-looking little man cherished as Charles Lamb and the regal graybeard who is King Lear. Yet to some of us they have become inseparables. We cannot see the aged monarch on the stage, even when he is as well played as he is by Louis Calhern,* without thinking of Lamb. We cannot listen to him, especially when in the storm he must outthunder the thunder by shouting,

> *Blow, winds, and crack your cheeks! rage! blow!*
> *You cataracts and hurricanoes, spout, . . . (etc.)*

without hearing, above the fury of his roars or imprecations, the quiet voice of Elia.

And what is Lamb saying? He is explaining the loss the tragedy is bound to sustain when an attempt is made to reduce the grandeur of its spirit to physical terms. He is identifying

* *King Lear*, by William Shakespeare. Directed by John Houseman. Inci-dental music and songs by Marc Blitzstein. Production designed and lighted by Ralph Alswang. Costumes by Dorothy Jeakins. Presented by Robert L. Joseph and Alexander H. Cohen. With a cast including Louis Calhern, Arnold Moss, Norman Lloyd, Edith Atwater, Joseph Wiseman, Wesley Addy, Martin Gabel, Jo Van Fleet, Nina Foch, etc. At the National Theatre, New York City. Opened December 25, 1950.

Lear with the forces of nature and pointing out that his greatness lies in intellectual rather than corporal dimensions. He is contending that the grimaces, gestures, and vocal tones of an actor can no more hope to capture the inner dilemmas and majesty of the king than the "contemptible machinery" of the theatre can expect to mimic the terrors of the storm. He is phrasing, with the magic that was his, the sense of diminishment which every responsive reader of *King Lear* is fated to experience when he encounters the play behind the footlights.

As I say, Elia must be listed among the speaking characters in the current revival in spite of the fact that it is by far the best New York has seen in my time. Mr. Calhern makes his valiant attempts to drown Lamb out and succeeds in doing so at many moments. It is in the storm scene where he fails completely. There the more he strains his vocal cords to release the roar of the tempestuous speeches, the more audible Elia becomes. This is not surprising. It is the expected proof of the play's power, hence of Lamb's rightness.

No actor I know of or have read about could hope to do justice to

> *Rumble thy bellyful! Spit, fire! spout, rain!*
> *Nor rain, wind, thunder, fire, are my*
> *daughters,* . . . (*etc.*)

Such eruptions are beyond the capacities of mortal throats and lungs. In them the Lear who addresses the elements directly speaks not as a man but as an element himself. The storm within him is as violent as the storm about him. For the sake of players, playgoers, and the play it would therefore seem an act of merciful wisdom to leave the impossible untried by avoiding these tirades in the theatre, or at least cutting them drastically. Readers can hear them when they are unspoken and their wild fury beats only upon the mind. When uttered, however, they lose their grandeur. The shouts they invite cannot suggest their needed volume. They are condemned to emerge as somewhat ludicrous confessions of human inadequacy.

What is noteworthy about Mr. Calhern's Lear is not that he fails in these speeches which are beyond successful speaking but that elsewhere he so often succeeds where so many Lears have failed. In the storm he may be no more than "the old man tottering about the stage with a walking-stick" that Lamb described. In most of the other scenes, however, his skill and power are such that even the most devoted Elians are forced to wonder if Lamb, instead of insisting categorically that "the Lear of Shakespeare cannot be acted," should not have qualified his statement to read *"all* of the Lear of Shakespeare cannot be acted."

The ultimate vastness of the text may, because of its very scale and kind, resist presentation. It is too towering, too turbulent and elemental to take mortal shape. It will always say to the reader something soaring yet intangible about human meanness and human vanity, about treachery, cruelty, a grief-broken mind, stout loyalty, and shining tenderness, which it cannot hope to say to the playgoer regardless of how well it is done. Even so, as the present revival makes excitingly clear, the tragedy's greatness, though in whittled form, can be captured behind the footlights. Its magnificence can at least be hinted at, and some of its terrible tensions projected.

If as playgoers we are unprepared for this, it is as much because of the weakness of the Lears to which we have been exposed as it is to the strength of Lamb's argument or the merits of the current production. When it comes to Lears, England has been luckier than America since the century's turn. Although of recent years London has had the privilege of seeing Olivier and Gielgud as the King, we have had to content ourselves with such a British visitor as Donald Wolfit. The Americans we remember in the part are Robert Mantell, Fritz Leiber, and Sam Jaffe. None of their monarchs was really distinguished, Mr. Jaffe's was pitiably inadequate, and all appeared in revivals which were less than pedestrian.

On the whole Mr. Calhern is as fortunate in the production in which he finds himself as it is in having him as its dominant figure. John Houseman's direction, which is swift-moving and intelligent, is alert to the script's theatrical possibilities no less than to its problems. Ralph Alswang's settings have the strength of their simplicity and are proper backgrounds for the savagery of a druidical Britain. They are lighted so that a changing switchboard scores the performance even as does Marc Blitzstein's music. Although the company is unfortunately weak in the Regan of Jo Van Fleet and possesses in Edith Atwater a Goneril of mild malevolence, it includes an admirable Kent in Martin Gabel, an effective Edmund in Joseph Wiseman, a pleasing Cordelia in Nina Foch, a touching Fool in Norman Lloyd, a sympathetic Edgar in Wesley Addy, and an excellent Gloucester in Arnold Moss, who is one of the best Shakespearean actors we have.

The pivotal point—the globe *and* Atlas—of any attempt to bring the tragedy to the stage is, of course, the actor who undertakes Lear. Mr. Calhern cannot have approached the challenge blindly. He must have known he was inviting a fiasco or a triumph. For this very reason he can be proud that the result has not been a fiasco.

Beyond Prose

No career in the contemporary theatre has taken a more en-
couraging turn than Mr. Calhern's since the war. 'Way back
in 1925 as the returned diplomat in Philip Barry's *In a Garden*
and a year later as Eilert Lovborg to Emily Stevens's *Hedda*
he stood out as a young player of exceptional promise. Thereafter, however, for some time he seemed to lose his way. His
luck in scripts was bad. His performances became perfunctory.
They were slick, trivial, superficial.

The change came when he toured in *Life with Father* and
was the most satisfactory of all the elder Days I saw. His
Tadeusz in *Jacobowsky and the Colonel* in 1944 was a brilliant
job carried off with great flourish and style. It was topped two
seasons later by the distinction of his Mr. Justice Holmes in
The Magnificent Yankee. Since then Mr. Calhern has demonstrated his suavity and precision in such a frothy comedy as *The Play's the Thing* and won a host of new admirers in such films as *Annie Get Your Gun* and *The Asphalt
Jungle*.

Certainly Buffalo Bill in *Annie Get Your Gun* is not the
homework one might expect for King Lear. For that matter,
neither is Clarence Day, Colonel Tadeusz, or Mr. Justice
Holmes. Each of these parts as played by Mr. Calhern has
been a further demonstration of his versatility and a new proof
of the thoroughness with which he has mastered the all-round
job of being an exceptionally good actor. Nonetheless, the
transition from prose to Shakespearean verse and from such
parts to King Lear, of all Shakespearean roles, can only be
described as a leap rather than a step. It must have required
genuine courage.

Fortunately this courage has proved not to be foolhardy.
Mr. Calhern has fine endowments to bring to Lear. That he is

six feet three inches tall in no way subtracts from the stature of his King. His monarch is a prepossessing figure, regal in carriage and enormous in dignity. There is in him something of the dynamic power of Michelangelo's Moses. This power grows throughout the evening. Although Mr. Calhern may start by reading almost too colloquially, he soon demonstrates how thoroughly he knows what he is up to. He resists the temptation, which must be strong, to release his voice to the utmost when upbraiding those "unnatural hags" who are Goneril and Regan. He does not fall into the common error of committing all his reserves before he must attack the scene on the heath. If in those speeches already referred to even his full voice proves insufficient, the simple, stubborn, Elian fact is that these outbursts are beyond mortal delivery.

Once this hurdle is passed Mr. Calhern succeeds to a degree I would not have dreamed possible in proving that Lear is a part which can be acted. His scenes with the Fool, Edgar, and Kent, when his reason has tottered and he is "cut to the brains," are touching in their mixture of madness, childlike sweetness, and sudden angry recollections of power. He reads beautifully the exquisite speech to Cordelia in which the King, contemplating their life in prison, says:

> . . . *we'll live,*
> *And pray, and sing, and tell old tales, and laugh*
> *At gilded butterflies, and hear poor rogues*
> *Talk of court news; and we'll talk with them too,*
> *Who loses and who wins, who's in, who's out;*
> *And take upon's the mystery of things,*
> *As if we were God's spies: and we'll wear out,*
> *In a wall'd prison, packs and sects of great ones*
> *That ebb and flow by the moon.*

Moreover, Mr. Calhern is magnificent in the majesty of his death. His "foolish, fond old man" dies as so bruised and baffled a victim of life that one would have to hate him indeed who "would upon the rack of this tough world/Stretch him out longer." If, in spite of the excellences of Mr. Calhern's performance and the merits of the present revival, Lamb still insists upon making himself heard, the fault is no one's except Shakespeare's. Mr. Calhern and his associates must be congratulated upon having communicated to the extent they have the vastness of a tragedy so storm-shaken in its emotions and filled with "the mystery of things" that its final greatness can never be confined on a stage.

January 20, 1951

*THE BUSINESS of poetry and poetry
as a business, with special reference to
Olivia de Havilland's prose Juliet and
T. S. Eliot's theories about dramatic
verse.*

When Words Sing

*I do not love thee, Doctor Fell,
The reason why I cannot tell;
But this alone I know full well,
I do not love thee, Doctor Fell.*

WHEN it comes to people, our likes and dislikes often defy rationalization. We explain them unscientifically by making vague references to chemistry. But let money be involved, let an expensive enterprise flounder financially, and hindsight can produce almost automatically a goodly list of reasons to make clear why what had meant to succeed was doomed to failure.

As a case in point take the elaborate production of *Romeo and Juliet* * in which Olivia de Havilland has been appearing. When its closing was announced, the expected explanations

* *Romeo and Juliet*, by William Shakespeare. Staged by Peter Glenville. Scenery and costumes by Oliver Messel. Incidental music by David Diamond. Choreography for pavan by George Balanchine. Presented by the late Dwight Deere Wiman. With a cast including Douglas Watson, Olivia de Havilland, Jack Hawkins, James Hayter, Evelyn Varden, Isobel Elsom, Robert Duke, Herbert Ransom, Malcolm Keen, William Smithers, Dorothy Pattern, etc. At the Broadhurst Theatre, New York City. Opened March 10, 1951.

were offered. Since they had to do with expenses, they were beyond dispute. Instead of being profitable, the six-weeks' tour before the New York opening had added alarmingly to an initial investment already sizable. The weekly receipts on Broadway, though above average, were below the formidable operating costs. The cast included twenty-two actors, many of them high-salaried, and fifteen extras. Twenty-five stagehands were required to move Oliver Messel's needlessly heavy settings. Seven musicians and three stage managers did not lessen an overhead so considerable that even players willing to accept cuts could not make the budget workable.

These were among the reasons given. Although having to do with business, as examples of economic planning they scarcely make the theatre seem businesslike. Nor do they touch upon what I suspect to have been the real reason why business at the box office was not all that had been dreamed of.

That reason? Poetry, or rather the lack of it, in the speaking of the lines in this *Romeo and Juliet*. To big executives the absence of poetry may appear the most unlikely of causes for running in the red. A thrombosis would no doubt overtake them were they to find poetry listed on a corporation's balance sheet. To *Romeo and Juliet*, however, Shakespeare's music is more than an asset. It is the play's real business. Its excuse and glory, too. Its full, unashamed release is the major source of the mood created and the pleasure given. If the poetry is muffled, silenced, or ignored, the tragedy is undone. Its enchantment is destroyed; its hot young passion reduced to ashes.

There were actors in this *Romeo and Juliet* who were competent enough. Evelyn Varden, for example, was a colorful Nurse. Malcolm Keen characterized his Capulet sharply. And, as far as the eyes go, Douglass Watson was a more satisfying young Montague than is usually seen. His Romeo also had the advantage of being blessed with an admirable intensity. But (and here was a tragedy unanticipated by Shakespeare), with the exception of Jack Hawkins's Mercutio, no one in the cast had the ability to do justice to Shakespeare's score. For that matter, Mr. Hawkins was the only one who seemed to realize that when Shakespeare wrote his tale of piteous misadventure he was functioning as a dramatist who was also an incomparable poet.

Certainly neither of the star-crossed lovers permitted us to rejoice in this fact. Although Mr. Watson plainly had his moments when he wanted to let the verse sing, his training in the delivery of poetry did not appear sufficient to enable him to follow his inclinations. True fervor lay behind his playing. Yet the melody he gave us was, so to speak, picked out with one finger. As for Miss de Havilland, her Juliet suffered from many lacks, including the fatal one of being uninteresting. Youthful looking though she was, she was without rapture; without variety, too; a prose Juliet who could close and lock the keyboard even on what one would have thought was the self-playing music of her speeches in the balcony scene.

Whether T. S. Eliot would share my laments at having actors smother the poetry in such a play as *Romeo and Juliet* I do not know. Recently I have been reading, and rereading, his *Poetry and Drama*,* that lecture he delivered at Harvard last November which is now available in book form. Many of the points he makes are familiar. Some of them find him repeating simple truisms so that they sound like difficult discoveries. All of them are trenchantly phrased by a man embarked earnestly

* *Poetry and Drama*, by T. S. Eliot. Cambridge: Harvard University Press. 44 pp. $1.50.

upon an admirable quest. But one of the arguments which he, as a poet, stresses about poetic drama finds me in open mutiny rather than in mild disagreement with him.

Mr. Eliot is a critic who during his past thirty, highly articulate years has been constantly attracted to dramatic literature. As the author of such well-known plays in verse as *Murder in the Cathedral, The Family Reunion,* and *The Cocktail Party,* he is, too, a creator who is still seeking to find a verse idiom suitable for dramatic expression in our own times.

No one could be more candid or disarming than he on the subject of his own experiments. He freely admits that in *Murder in the Cathedral* he failed to solve any general problem, relied too often upon the choral interludes, and reached from his own point of view what was no more than a "dead end." *The Family Reunion,* as he reconsiders it, was "defective" because of containing too many passages which "could not be dramatically justified." The source of *The Cocktail Party,* which none of his friends and none of the dramatic critics recognized, was, he confesses, the *Alcestis* of Euripides. "It is," he adds, "perhaps an open question whether there is any poetry in the play at all."

Somewhat tardily Mr. Eliot has come to the conclusion that, to justify itself theatrically, verse must be more than merely fine poetry shaped into dramatic form and that "no play should be written in verse for which prose is dramatically adequate." But I do think his theory carries him away when he insists that the duty of the dramatic poet is "to accustom our audiences to verse to the point at which they will cease to be conscious of it."

He indulges in an equally odd overstatement, I believe, when he endeavors to maintain that a spectator, seeing *Hamlet* for the first time, would be so swept away by its story that he would be unaware of the glories of its poetic diction. In my opinion he is no less open to rebuttal when he contends that "what we have to do is to bring poetry into the world in which the audience lives and to which it returns when it leaves the theatre; not to transport the audience into some imaginary world totally unlike their own, an unreal world in which poetry can be spoken."

Beyond question Mr. Eliot's "ascetic" rule to avoid poetry which would call attention to itself as poetry was triumphantly obeyed when in *The Cocktail Party* he wrote such a speech as:

> *And so will you send me to the sanatorium?*
> *I can't go home again. And at my club*
> *They won't let you keep a room for more than*
> *   seven days;*
> *I haven't the courage to go to a hotel,*
> *And besides, I need more shirts—you can get my*
> *   wife*
> *To have my things sent on: whatever I shall need.*
> *But of course you mustn't tell her where I am.*
> *Is it far to go?*

No wonder audiences do not recognize such an utterance as verse. It is poetry merely by the printer's courtesy. But what about such famous lines as Juliet's?

> *O, swear not by the moon, th' inconstant moon,*
> *That monthly changes in her circled orb,*
> *Lest that thy love prove likewise variable.*

Obviously no girl of fourteen or woman of any age was ever able, in what is hazily identified as real life, to summon such language when smiling at her suitor's vows of affection. A supreme poet, and at that only one poet who also happened to

· 109 ·

be a supreme playwright, was capable of writing such a speech and persuading us that not only Juliet could have said this but that all people in love should face the moonlight with such words.

The paradox of Mr. Eliot's position is that he is at once tinglingly aware and bravely in search of what a poetic drama has "potentially to offer the playgoer that prose drama cannot." He knows that dramatic poetry gives expression to a "peculiar range of sensibility . . . at its moments of greatest intensity." At such moments, he adds, we touch the border of those feelings which only music can express.

I follow him completely when he mentions emotions which only music can express. I must admit, however, I cannot follow him at all when he seems to be pleading that as theatregoers we should not be allowed to be conscious of the fact that the music to which we are listening is dramatic poetry. I, no more than Mr. Eliot, want poetic dramas which are written by poets who are not dramatists. I, no more than he, wish to listen in the presence of a play to fine poetry which is out of character, which calls attention to itself only for its own sake, and has no relation either to the mood or action. Yet I do insist, and this is where I part company with both Mr. Eliot and the recent production of *Romeo and Juliet,* that I feel cheated if, as written and spoken, the speeches in a poetic play do not provide me with pleasures and excitements manifestly beyond the range and intention of the dialogue in such plays as *Dead End, Hedda Gabler,* or even *The Cherry Orchard.*

When a poetic dramatist has mastered, as he must, the twin arts of poetry and the drama, I think actors do him (and their audiences) a cruel injustice if they deny him the music which gives his drama wings. To be ashamed of poetry, to have it spoken as if it were prose, seems to me as disappointing as it would be to go hoping to hear Flagstad sing and then have her talk.

No one wants declamation in the old tawdry and overblown sense of the word. Words that sing, however, are quite another matter. They must not be denied their song. It creates not only a pleasure but a world apart. It is a world in which both this world and the theatre acquire new depths and dimensions. Although Juliet may wish, for understandable reasons, that Romeo could doff his name, there is no reason that I can comprehend why the poetic drama should have its poetry stifled. Perhaps, if Mr. Eliot had listened to Shakespeare's verse as Miss de Havilland and Mr. Watson robbed it of its melody and reduced it to prose, he would be as anxious as I am to allow audiences to share *consciously* in the delights which only genuine dramatic verse can supply when proudly spoken as the glorious creation it is.

April 28, 1951

THE EXPOSURE of Macbeth *to a weird "reading" by Dr. Edith Sitwell, tented in brocade, or a demonstration of how much better poetry sounds when read by players rather than poets.*

꿈꿈꿈꿈꿈꿈꿈꿈꿈꿈꿈꿈꿈꿈꿈꿈꿈꿈꿈꿈꿈꿈꿈꿈꿈꿈꿈

Poets and Players

MACBETH and *The Lady's Not for Burning* * would, you might think, be safely beyond coupling. The one is all terror, horror, and decline; the other is all, or almost all, bounce, fooling, and gaiety. At first it might seem that the two of them have no more in common than the fact that Englishmen wrote them and wrote them in verse. In spite of the centuries and endowments separating them, Shakespeare's tragedy and Christopher Fry's comedy share, however, another feature equally obvious and equally important. Both were written for the theatre; both, in other words, were meant to be given the benefit of a production and to be spoken by actors.

What leads me to bracket two plays so dissimilar is that within a few days' time I chanced to sit before them as they were being performed in very different ways under very differ-

* *The Lady's Not for Burning*, a romantic comedy by Christopher Fry. Directed by John Gielgud. Setting by Oliver Messel. Presented by Atlantis Productions (The Theatre Guild, Tennent Productions Ltd., John C. Wilson). With John Gielgud, Pamela Brown, Richard Burton, Penelope Munday, David Evans, Nora Nicholson, Richard Leech, George Howe, Eliot Makeham, Peter Bull, and Esme Percy. At the Royale Theatre. New York City. Opened November 8, 1950.

ent circumstances. *Macbeth* * was being subjected to a recital or a reading (call it what you will) by Dr. Edith Sitwell at the Museum of Modern Art, and *The Lady's Not for Burning* was being acted in a regular theatre by such superior professionals as John Gielgud and Pamela Brown. The question raised not only by these methods of presentation but by Monroe Wheeler's introduction of Dr. Edith was whether poets or actors can do greater justice to the words of a poetic dramatist.

Mr. Wheeler, the Museum's director, told us that Dr. Edith had always dreamed of performing *Macbeth* "in one way or another." Her intention was to give a poet's conception of Shakespeare's dramatic verse. That she had had no training as an actress was, one gathered, a mark in her favor since Mr. Wheeler next proceeded to comment on the bad eloquence of actors. With a good deal of relish Mr. Wheeler told the story of how Dr. Johnson had once corrected Garrick's misreading of his lines and had further offended him by insisting "the players, Sir, have got a kind of rant, with which they run on, without any regard either to accent or emphasis." Considering what was to come, such a prelude seemed in the nature of a calculated risk.

The morning dress rehearsal of this *Macbeth*, which I attended, was an experience I shall not soon forget. Although ostensibly given for the working press, the audience was composed mainly of those worshipful followers Dr. Edith and Sir Osbert Sitwell have won for themselves in New York. No incense was burned, yet the scent of it seemed to hang heavy

---

* *Macbeth*, by William Shakespeare. Recital of scenes by Dr. Edith Sitwell, assisted by Glenway Wescott, Bernard Savage, and Gertrude Flynn. Presented by the Trustees of the Museum of Modern Art on November 16, 1950.

in the air, because those who know the Sitwells love them with a love which is utter adoration.

At a few minutes past eleven Dr. Edith's three assistants trooped down the aisle and took their places at a long table to the left of the stage. These assistants included Glenway Wescott, the novelist, who also enjoyed the assumed advantage of not being a member of Equity, and Bernard Savage and Gertrude Flynn, two professionals who had their courage with them.

Mr. Wescott, the recital's Macbeth, was innocent of the horned helmet, heavy armor, and kilts favored by tradition. He wore a dinner jacket. So did Mr. Savage, who served as a sort of accommodator, capable of changing without batting an eye from Banquo to the Doctor. Miss Flynn, a pretty young woman condemned to sit like Patience on a monument until she appeared as the Gentlewoman in the sleep-walking scene, wore a gray evening dress. These three helpers seated themselves behind microphones and glasses of water. And there they sat, looking for all the world as if they were engaged in a Prohibitionist production of *The Cocktail Party*, until Dr. Edith made her entrance.

The entrance she made was a considerable one. Preceded by Mr. Wheeler, she moved through the darkened auditorium like a priestess approaching a pagan altar. She was tall, turbaned, and impressive, a figure deserving reverence and expecting it. It was only when she appeared under the platform's lights, pale of face, queenly, and acknowledging with upturned, swallowlike flights of her beautiful hands the applause of her devotees, that it was possible to appreciate the splendor of her singularity. It was only then, too, that the rich brocade in which she was tented could be appreciated.

Soon thereafter she sat down to the right of the stage, a personage mysterious and mighty, until with a poet's proper defiance of period details she opened a very modern black handbag, reached for a very modern handkerchief, blew her nose, and covered her fine but small and piercing eyes with some very modern horn-rimmed spectacles. While Mr. Wheeler was providing his challenging overture to the promised music, Dr. Edith occupied herself arranging the voluminous folds of her heavy brocade gown. As she sat there waiting, it was hard to tell, in the irreverent words of a neighbor of mine, whether she was covering a teapot or a telephone.

When Mr. Wheeler left the stage Dr. Edith, whose voice he had described as "the most beautiful in the world," began her recital. This consisted partly of reading scenes from *Macbeth* with the aid of her assistants and partly of Dr. Edith's own analysis of Shakespeare's poetry and meaning. No one who has read *A Poet's Notebook* or the chapters therefrom which first appeared in *The Atlantic* can question Dr. Edith's devotion to Shakespeare, her poet's insight into his technical devices, or the occasional grandeur of her own language when seeking to explain Shakespeare. No temptation to laugh, no awareness of what was pretentious to the point of freakishness in the whole proceedings, however, could quite destroy the illusion in those outfront that this extraordinary woman, who has created her own mythology, might very well be on speaking terms with the sibyls.

It seems equally certain that Shakespeare would never have recognized himself in the poet by that name she was dissecting. He might have been interested to learn that some of his words, as his tragedy progressed, were "rusty as though they had lain in the blood that had been spilt." Human vanity being what it is, he would no doubt have been touched by her dedication to him and pleased by the liturgical quality of her praise. But so overintellectualized was Dr. Edith's approach to what Shakespeare did instinctively that in all probability he would have been befuddled by her prating about "schemes of tuneless, dropping dissonances," "a thickened, darkened assonance," and his "placing of double-syllabled and treble-syllabled words and quick-moving, unaccented, one-syllabled words." My own suspicion is that such highfalutin talk would have caused Shakespeare to outlaugh Little Audrey.

Now to Dr. Edith's recital of such scenes and speeches as she had selected. A lecture is one thing, a play another. The two do not mix. No drama can be expected to survive if it is cut up into canapés, and if critical comments are always interrupting the line of its action and destroying its suspense. The supposed justification of this hodge-podge treatment of Shakespeare's tragedy was, as I have hinted, to let us hear his poet's words spoken by a poet. As it turned out, this proved to be a poetic fallacy, if ever there was one. That Dr. Edith has an arresting voice, no one can deny. But that she has scant knowledge of how to use it dramatically seems equally incontestable. Reading with an ear for assonance rather than an eye for character, she succeeded chiefly in reducing Lady Macbeth to a lesson in prosody.

Most of us when we sing hymns are apt to adopt an astral quaver, devotional and thin, which has nothing in common with our voices as we release them out of church. Dr. Edith's reading of Shakespeare was done in what I assume is her "poetry voice"—a voice quite different from the one she employed on her own text. It was all boom and incantation, less designed for dialogue than for a Gregorian chant.

Oddly enough, it was lacking in any emphasis except a maintained and indiscriminate overemphasis. Even at the fearful moments of the planning and carrying out of Duncan's murder it refused to subside into a whisper. Throughout the morning Dr. Edith was so anxious to do justice to all the technical subtleties of Shakespeare's verse that she ended by doing dramatic justice to none. She followed vocally the course of the cargo ship in *Mister Roberts,* and made trips from Tedium to Monotony and back again.

Mr. Wescott, who has a deep and agreeable voice even if his "r's" are resolutely loyal to Kewaskum, Wis., stood up from time to time to read Macbeth with manifest affection, and no doubt commendably enough by classroom standards. I know, however, I was grateful (and I do not think I was alone) whenever Mr. Savage spoke as only a trained actor can. I know, too, that I could have cheered when at overlong last Miss Flynn was given a chance to speak, and spoke admirably, the lines of the Gentlewoman. I would never have believed that so insignificant a part could become the stellar role in *Macbeth.* Yet this is precisely what happened during Dr. Edith's "recital," and must be taken as the measure of its failure.

Granting that *The Lady's Not for Burning* is as different from *Macbeth* as teatime is from midnight, the sheer relief of having actors in the cast to deliver Mr. Fry's verse (in the sense of acting rather than reading it) was supreme. Since the time of Plato's *Ion,* if not before, actors have occupied a dubious position in the hierarchy of artists. Many critics have been unwilling to admit them to the ranks of true creators inasmuch as, since they usually speak lines written by someone else, they are interpreters of an interpreter. This is often held to give them a secondary status.

However, Dr. Edith's recital, in which Shakespeare was murdered along with Duncan and Banquo, persuades me actors are grievously underestimated. Having listened with enchantment to the ease, sparkle, authority, and variety with which Mr. Gielgud and Miss Brown project Mr. Fry's sprightly lines, I know that I for one will turn cottoned ears to all lyre-strummers deluded enough to believe that poets are the best readers of poetry and actors mere sounding boards for the sensibilities of others.

Christopher Fry is a Britisher of forty-three who, within the year, has won and deserved international attention. As everyone must know who has seen *The Lady's Not for Burning*, or read it, *A Phoenix Too Frequent*, or *Venus Observed*, his is one of the most exciting talents the postwar theatre has yielded. Under Attlee's prosaic government, in a theatre made brackish by its realism, and during times aggressively unlyrical, he has triumphed as a poetic dramatist.

Mr. Fry has invited straphangers, accustomed to traveling on the subway, to take a ride on Pegasus. More than that, he has made them like it. "What a wonderful thing is a metaphor," cries the hero in *The Lady's Not for Burning*. Plainly Mr. Fry agrees with him. He loves the language. He uses it with a glorious profligacy. He thinks, sees, smells, and tastes in terms of verbal images.

Whether he is writing about a British nobleman's decision to have his son choose a wife for him (*Venus Observed*), dramatizing Petronius's tale of the Ephesian widow who, when preparing to die in her husband's tomb, falls in love with a guard (*A Phoenix Too Frequent*), or telling, as in *The Lady*, the story of a soldier who upsets a village by pretending to want to be hanged in order to save a young girl suspected of witchcraft, metaphors and similes come galloping from his pen so fast that they almost trip over one another. That Mr. Fry over-writes is undeniable. But that he can write with shimmering magic is equally and delectably apparent.

Most people today have been fed for so long upon a thin porridge of prose in the theatre that they have almost lost a taste for listening. Mr. Fry's verse makes its uncompromising demands on the ears. To be fully relished, *The Lady* should perhaps be read before it is seen—and heard. Even then it can at moments prove exhausting. This exhaustion, however, is in itself pleasant inasmuch as it is brought about by the richness rather than the poverty of Mr. Fry's talent.

The Lady is a comedy in which the laughter, in typical Fry fashion, is interrupted from time to time by sudden stabs of disenchantment. Its spirit, nonetheless, is essentially ebullient. It is as full of bravura as if Dick Dudgeon in *The Devil's Dis-ciple* and the braggart Irishman of *The Playboy of the Western World* had been merged into one character.

If Mr. Fry's shimmering lines were exposed to a "poetry voice," his play would die an abrupt and painful death. Mr. Gielgud and Miss Brown are, of course, at once too wise and expert to smother it in this manner. So are such of their associ-ates in an admirable cast as Richard Burton and Eliot Make-ham. All of these players are masters of their profession. They know how to bring out the song in a poetic speech and give it style at the same time that they keep it conversational. They read precisely, with an unflagging instinct for emphasis and a superb sense of pace and variety. Poets they may not be, but skilful actors they are. For this very reason the poetry they speak gains rather than suffers as it leaves their lips.

December 2, 1950

THAT DELIGHTFULLY anachronistic fellow, Christopher Fry, who has wandered from one Elizabethan age into another, and a contrast between his talents and T. S. Eliot's.

Yes and No

YEARS ago when I published a critical appraisal of the American theatre called *Upstage,* a reviewer in the *New Republic* summarized his objections to it by heading his notice, "Mr. Brown Says Yes and No." If I never cringed under this rebuke as much as I was meant to, it was because the business of criticism as I saw it then—and see it now—is not a matter of ecstatic "Yes's" or thundering "No's."

The easiest reviews to write are those written from the heat of either extreme admiration or extreme disapproval. Every reviewer knows this; every reader senses it, too. But criticism, if it involves judgment at all and hence speaks for the mind no less than the emotions, is usually bound to have its reservations in the midst of praise and to recognize that merits can exist along with faults.

Certainly no play produced this year makes a mixture of "Yes's" and "No's" more inevitable than Christopher Fry's *Venus Observed.** Mr. Fry is blessed with one of the most de-

* *Venus Observed,* by Christopher Fry. Directed by Laurence Olivier. Settings by Roger Furse. Music by Herbert Menges. Costumes for Miss Palmer by Valentina, others by Mildred Trebor. Presented by the Theatre Guild by

lightful talents now contributing to the theatre. He has a wit, nimble and original; an agile and unpredictable mind, as playful as it is probing; and a love of language which can only be described as a lust.

If no one else writes as he does, it is because he approaches life, death, the world around him, the theatre, the thesaurus, and the dictionary in a way which is very much his own. He is an anachronism, if you will; a fellow who has wandered from one Elizabethan age into another. The Mermaid Tavern he has reopened in contemporary Mayfair may not serve the beef it used to. Yet something of the earlier Elizabethan vigor is there, the old dash and exuberance, the "fine madness," the worship of the metaphor, the lack of fear in beauty's presence, and the unrationed indulgence in words and phrases for the mere melodious sport to be had from them.

Perhaps it is this faintly Elizabethan quality in Mr. Fry which makes his virtues more at home in a costume comedy about the past, such as *The Lady's Not for Burning*, than they are in *Venus Observed*, which is laid in the present. The beauties remain. The wit is no less shimmering. The imagination is as unfettered and unfettering as ever. But some of the mannerisms grow irritating. The excesses, always a little wearing, prove the more fatiguing. The limitations call attention to themselves along with the delights.

Few people could approach the writing of drama in verse more differently than T. S. Eliot and Mr. Fry. Where Mr. Eliot has accustomed us to the bones of poetry, beautiful but

---

arrangement with Laurence Olivier Productions, Ltd. With Rex Harrison, Lilli Palmer, John Williams, Claudia Morgan, Eileen Peel, Joan Haythorne, John Merivale, James Westerfield, Stuart Burge, and Hurd Hatfield. At the Century Theatre, New York City. Opened February 13, 1952.

often bleached by scrupulous editing, Mr. Fry concentrates on all the sensuous splendors of the flesh, ignoring the skeleton of sustained ideas or dramatic structure. To change the image, Mr. Eliot's restraint is such that he sometimes closes the piano before playing it, embarrassed by the music it might release and wanting dramatic poetry to pass as prose until the igniting moment for its justification has come. The pleasure Mr. Fry has, and gives, is quite different. He likes to tickle and caress the keyboard. Although his touch is wonderfully light, when he is playing the English language the delight he supplies comes from his letting everyone know that he is doing so.

In *Venus Observed* Mr. Fry is writing about an aging duke who wants to marry again, and asks his son to choose his new wife for him. The duke, who has been in as much circulation as a popular novel in a lending library, is ready to forget his "vintage years of love" and resign himself to monogamy. The three candidates are attractive women who have already been part of his "joyous routine." Before this judgment of Paris can be made both the duke and his son fall in love with the young daughter of their family agent. The duke, a star-gazer by inclination, is brought down to human concerns and worries by having his observatory burned by one of the three older women.

In the process of exposing the duke to reality, Mr. Fry writes impishly, brilliantly, and beautifully about many things, including the contrasts between youth and age. Where his mood in *The Lady's Not for Burning* was springlike, in *Venus Observed* it is autumnal. Beneath the dialogue's bubbling gaiety and underlying both its sense and nonsense there is a strong note of melancholy.

What Mr. Fry's play actually means in each and all of its madcap twists, I do not pretend to know. But I do know that it has been agreeably set by Roger Furse; that it is admirably played throughout, especially by John Williams as the dishonest but lovable old steward and Lilli Palmer who is charming as his daughter; and that Rex Harrison reads the most difficult speeches as if they were easy and is the master of every scene in which he appears.

If the performances are so good and the text is so filled with the felicities of Mr. Fry's writing, why should any "No's" creep into a review of *Venus Observed* to offset the "Yes's"? For one thing, the Century Theatre is too large for the delicate values of Mr. Fry's style. The vastness of the auditorium denies the script its needed intimacy. It also adds to the difficulties of following Mr. Fry's verses which, under the most favorable circumstances, require the closest listening.

Mr. Fry is not a dramatist to keep his feet on the sober earth. In his phrase, he delights himself—and us—by "coruscating on thin ice." His fancy is never still. It is sudden in its twists and arrowlike in its flights. A play by him is not so much a play as it is what he calls "an act of poetry." The fun comes from his saying the usual thing in the unusual way (as, for example, translating "released from jail" into "disengaged from custody"). It comes from the unfailing lilt and often magical beauty of his verses. It is a product of a riot of images. It is the result of our awareness that Mr. Fry is not only writing but overwriting shamelessly, deliriously, ecstatically. He knows this as well as we do, and spoofs his fondness for words in that sentence, a tongue-twister if there ever was one, which Miss Palmer reads triumphantly in spite of its being forty-four lines long.

The evening's real disappointment runs deeper. In *Venus Observed* the same Mr. Fry who charms our ears also tires them. He gives us more than we can take and yet less than we want. His words, beguiling as they are, lack substance. We feel pleased and cheated at the same time. Far worse than suffering verbally from too much of a muchness, *Venus Observed* ends up by suffering humanly from too much of a littleness. Its brightness cannot hide its emptiness, and that emptiness finally becomes enervating.

March 1, 1952

Star Bright

A BRIEF but magical stage cross by Alfred Lunt, which shows how a servant can be a master of the style, elegance, and wit needed to do justice to Mozart.

㿟㿟㿟㿟㿟㿟㿟㿟㿟㿟㿟㿟㿟㿟㿟㿟㿟㿟㿟㿟㿟㿟㿟㿟㿟㿟㿟㿟㿟㿟

Lighting More Than Candles

THE LAST entry in the cast for *Cosi fan tutte*, as printed in the Metropolitan's program, reads, "A servant . . . Alfred Lunt." That is all. And all Mr. Lunt has to do, in what for him is a new domestic capacity, is to cross the stage, taper in hand, and pretend to light ten hooded electric fixtures which are doing some pretending of their own, since they are masquerading as the kind of footlights Mozart might have known. When the last candle is lighted and Mr. Lunt has crossed the stage in utter silence, he vanishes into the wings, not to appear again. The singers and the orchestra thereupon take over. Yet somehow Mr. Lunt, though absent, manages to remain present for the rest of a delightful evening.

Mr. Lunt apparently will play this mute flunkey for no more than four or five performances. Then his introductory business, indulged in as a lark, will be dropped and the overture lead straight into the score. Although the evening's rewards will continue to be abundant, something will be lost because Mr. Lunt's brief crossing is more than a personal appearance. It provides as vivid an illustration as can be found of the gifts he possesses which have enabled him to blend theatre with opera and hence light up the whole performance of *Cosi fan tutte* at the Metropolitan.

What makes Mr. Lunt's presence at the Met notable is that he appears there as an actor on a stage where singers are always plentiful and actors usually scarce. To watch him enter, cross, and exit is to sample the kind of lesson in acting which as a director he must have given his singers when he transformed them into players.

Mr. Lunt does not emerge; he makes an entrance, the sort of entrance only a real actor could make. The minute he steps into view the audience becomes a "captive audience." Plainly Mr. Lunt is not a person but a personage. Trying to behave as if he were nobody, he is beyond mistaking somebody. White-wigged, beruffled, wearing a smartly cut plum-colored coat, knee breeches, silk stockings, treading on high-heeled shoes, and flourishing a long taper in his right hand and a lace handkerchief in his left, he is the epitome of courtly elegance.

His immediate domination of the stage and auditorium, however, is not a matter of costume but of personality and technique. No one can fail to recognize that Mr. Lunt is completely at home behind the footlights. He is a master of his craft whose authority is such that he can be relaxed. He knows exactly what he wants to do and how he wants to do it, and proceeds to do it in precisely that fashion.

Does the importance of a part depend upon its length? Certainly not. A part, as Mr. Lunt proves, is as important as the actor who plays it. Can a silent man be witty? The answer is, of course, "Yes," if he happens to speak the language of pantomime with Mr. Lunt's eloquence. Without a word to say, Mr. Lunt converts the wavings of his taper into demonstrations of eighteenth-century decorum, the flourishes of his handkerchief into epigrams, and the grace of his movements into perfect patterns for the stance and stylization of Mozartian characters. Then, suddenly, the little that is so much is over, and Mr. Lunt is gone. But his spirit, his manner, and his wonderfully gay comic touch remain, brightening at every turn and in beguiling ways the performance of *Cosi fan tutte* he has staged.

Reviewers, always fallible in spite of all the ridiculous air of infallibility with which print curses their guesswork and reflexes, are never more unreliable or absurd than when they claim to be able to make a clear-cut distinction between acting and directing. Only those who have attended rehearsals have any way of knowing, as a rule, what an actor does because he thought of it himself and what he does because a director told him to do it. In the case of *Cosi,* however, Mr. Lunt's contributions are as self-evident as the skyscrapers of Manhattan on a cloudless day.

The most hackneyed complaints against opera are that, while it pretends to be music drama, it forgets the drama in the interests of the music; that it is the prisoner of static and silly conventions which destroy stage illusion; and that, though its singers, mountainous or willowy, can sing like nightingales, all too often they content themselves with acting like auks. A certain Corno di Bassetto, better known as Bernard Shaw, once pointed out "it is still possible for a prima donna to bounce on the stage and throw her voice at the heads of the audience with an insolent insistence on her position as a public favorite, and hardly the ghost of a reference to the character she is supposed to impersonate." That was in 1890, and the possibility remains possible even now. Rudolf Bing would be the first to admit this. As is proved by his turning to such theatre people as Margaret Webster, Garson Kanin, and Mr. Lunt for directors, Mr. Bing is determined that such a possibility will become an impossibility at the Met.

Certainly no one can complain that Eleanor Steber, Blanche Thebom, Patrice Munsel, Richard Tucker, Frank Guarrera, and John Brownlee fail to act in *Cosi fan tutte*. They not only act—they act like people who have had the privilege of being instructed in acting by Alfred Lunt. They seem as much at ease on the stage as he does. They are relaxed in his manner. They move about in the charming costumes and before the enchanting settings of Rolf Gerard with Mr. Lunt's elegance and style. They speak with his clarity and even employ his gestures. They appear to enjoy the comedy they are playing as much as he enjoyed romping through *O Mistress Mine*, *Amphitryon 38*, or *The Taming of the Shrew*. Their comic business is necessarily of a more courtly kind. But to their spoofing of the grand demeanor they bring Mr. Lunt's lighthearted- ness, flourish, and wit.

I happen to be one of those who find all operas, except *Carmen*, too long. Yet I must confess that the capable Luntlings in *Cosi fan tutte* not only added to my delight in Mozart's score but made me willing to forget the idiocies of Lorenzo da Ponte's libretto. My admiration for Mr. Lunt's share in the evening does not stop with his ability to turn singers into actors and opera into theatre. I am also amazed by the illusion his cast creates of having had months, instead of hours, of rehearsal and by the sense of intimacy he and Mr. Gerard establish on the Met's huge stage.

When Mr. Lunt consented to stage *Cosi fan tutte*, he admitted to the members of the Metropolitan Opera Guild that he felt rather like a groom at a shotgun wedding. "My intentions were honorable," he added. "I had never seen the girl before, though I knew several of her brothers, *Rigoletto* and *Figaro* among them." Shotgun or not, the result is one of the happiest of marriages.

January 16, 1952

AN AUTHOR, who was an actor at heart, is once more as successful on the boards as he was between them when one of his famous "readings" is re-created by Emlyn Williams.

≈≈≈≈≈≈≈≈≈≈≈≈≈≈≈≈≈≈≈≈≈≈≈≈≈≈≈≈≈≈≈≈≈≈≈

Mr. Dickens Reads Again

MANY people remember Mr. Crummles's admiration for the actor who was so thorough that, when he played Othello, he used to black himself all over. Just what Emlyn Williams does to prepare himself to appear as Charles Dickens * giving one of his famous "readings" has not as yet been revealed. But this much is certain. Mr. Williams has so steeped himself in Dickens and his works that those of us outfront could almost swear, were it not for the day's news tugging at our hearts and the look and dress of the audience around us, that in some magical manner we had been carried back in time and were listening to Dickens himself when in 1867–68, by doing precisely what Mr. Williams is doing, he scored a triumph in this country such as few performers have ever achieved.

Mr. Williams's success does not depend upon his making himself up to look like Dickens, upon his wearing evening clothes as dandified as Boz's were, upon his sporting the in-

* *Charles Dickens*, Emlyn Williams in a solo performance as Mr. Dickens "reading" scenes from his works. Presented by S. Hurok. At the John Golden Theatre, New York City. Opened February 4, 1952.

evitable boutonnière, or upon his using a desk which is a replica of the specially designed contraption Dickens evolved after long years of trial and error. These outward similarities, established by the make-up box, the tailor, and the carpenter, play, of course, a helpful part. The fun they provide would, however, be short-lived and of a childish kind, were Mr. Williams's evocation of a Dickens reading to stop with them. Fortunately these externals mark the beginning, not the end, of the evening's genuine and unusual pleasures.

Mr. Williams happens to be by training, temperament, and long employment what Dickens was only by temperament and inclination. He is an actor and an exceptional one, proud of his profession and unfrustrated in pursuing it. He is a playwright and a director, too. In fact, he is what Dickens always was at heart and finally became in public by giving readings—and that is, in Carlyle's phrase, "a whole tragic comic heroic *theatre* visible, performing under one *hat*."

No one was ever more stagestruck than Dickens. He was forever dabbling in amateur theatricals and hoping to find some noble cause or impoverished author to justify his getting up a benefit. The theatre was in his blood, in his nostrils, in his appearance, and in his pen. "I have often thought," he once confessed, "that I should certainly have been as successful on the boards as I have been between them." Convinced as he was of this, his ears must have greeted as music the words spoken to him at a rehearsal by a stage carpenter, "Ah, sir, it's a universal observation in the profession, sir, that it was a great loss to the public when you took to writing books." That Dickens agreed cannot be doubted since he ultimately made up for that loss by acting the books he had written.

His so-called "readings" were not literary programs. They

were theatrical performances of the most hypnotic kind, culled from his own works and projected as drama. If Dickens reveled in them, so did the thousands who crowded to see and hear him. To follow his tours, as reported by John Forster and Hesketh Pearson or in the exuberantly naive letters Dickens himself wrote home, is to read about an author who, whenever he appeared in his own country, Ireland, or America, in small towns or large cities, enjoyed the kind of adulation usually reserved for returning heroes or popular heads of states.

Dickens's successes, though spectacular, were monotonous in their regularity. He always had "a splendid hall." Tickets were always being snapped up after the opening of the box office by people who had stood in line the cold night through or formed queues early in the morning. Each program received an ovation. The only people dissatisfied were the grumbling multitudes unable to squeeze in. As surely as Dickens's ego had found its release on the stage, his purse had benefited. Pounds and dollars poured in at such an unprecedented rate that, after having read in public for twelve years, he left a net estate amounting to £93,000, almost half of which had been amassed from his readings.

These earnings and these triumphs, however fabulous, were not gained without great cost. Dickens's biographers agree that his life was shortened at least ten years because of the spent energies, the nervous strain, and the physical fatigues of his personal appearances and arduous travels. When he began his American tour after nine years of barnstorming in Great Britain, he was already a sick man and became sicker here. He was plagued with lameness in his left foot, with a weakened heart, and catarrh aggravated by standing on the cold platforms of

American railway coaches to escape from their overheated interiors.

Dickens was tired, too; a man who was maintaining at least a semblance of his extraordinary vitality by living on pills and who (in Forster's phrase) "unhappily . . . never thought of husbanding his strength except for the purpose of making fresh demands upon it." Nonetheless he came, was seen, and conquered. His conquest was so complete that Americans everywhere were willing to forget their anger at the hard things he had said about them and their culture twenty-five years before in *Martin Chuzzlewit* and *American Notes* after his first visit to the States.

How did he conquer? Dickens's performance, says Mr. Pearson * in a vivid paragraph based on contemporary observations, "could never properly be described as a reading, or himself as a reader. It was a highly theatrical representation by an actor who could impersonate any number of totally different characters and sink his own personality in each. He seemed to undergo physical transformation as he passed from one character to another, his voice, features, expressions, and mannerisms changing completely in a flash. He had a score of voices, male, female, old, young, middle-aged, cockney, yokel, military, naval, medical, clerical, forensic, aristocratic; and he had a score of faces. . . . His voice was naturally rich and deep, capable of every tone and half-tone, of quiet pathos, boisterous humor, martial ardor. But in addition to his vocal variety and his mimetic genius, there was in him beyond doubt a magnetic or mesmeric quality which enabled him to hold an audience, to play on its emotions, to make it laugh, cry, cheer, applaud, at his behest."

* *Dickens, His Character, Comedy and Career*, by Hesketh Pearson.

It would be hard to find a better description of what Mr. Williams does as Dickens than this description of what Dickens did himself. He, too, is able by the most telling suggestions to create a stageful of characters. He, too, has not one face but many faces, and an endless variety of voices. And he, too, by the mesmeric quality he possesses creates in an audience precisely the moods and responses the scene demands and he desires. Mr. Williams uses his body with amazing grace; his hands have an eloquence of their own. By lifting an eyebrow, by holding his head for an instant on one side, by suddenly altering his accent or tones, he sets and shapes a scene and makes transitions from character to character which are instantaneous and persuasive.

Mr. Williams divides his program into three sections of two scenes each. Starting with the Veneerings' comic party from *Our Mutual Friend,* he moves on for sentiment to Paul's death from *Dombey and Son.* After an intermission he continues with Bob Sawyer's hilarious bachelor party from *Pickwick Papers* and "The Signalman," an indifferent supernatural yarn from *Christmas Stories,* which he acts with great skill. Excellent as he is in these earlier sections, Mr. Williams is perhaps at his best in the drolly poignant episode, also from *Christmas Stories,* about Mr. Chops, the dwarf, who has his sad experience in Society. He ends the evening stirringly with an interlude about the heartless Monseigneur in *A Tale of Two Cities.*

It is perhaps odd that the one character Mr. Williams does not even bother to suggest is Mr. Pickwick. Devoted Dickensians may also find it strange that Mr. Williams has chosen to omit such of Dickens's own favorite impersonations as Mrs. Gamp, the trial scene in *Pickwick,* Nicholas Nickleby and Fanny Squeers, and his selection from the Steerforth part of

David Copperfield. Even so, there is infinite pleasure to be had from the program Mr. Williams presents and the way in which he presents it. Among other things there is the sheer joy to be had from the pictures summoned in sentence after sentence by the originality and vividness of Dickens's images. Take Mrs. Podsnap, for example, with her "quantity of bone, neck and nostrils like a rocking-horse," or old Lady Tippins "with an immense obtuse drab oblong face, like a face in a tablespoon."

Few people could give such depth to externalities as Dickens. Or, for that matter, match him in the pithiness of his incidental comments, as when he notes that Mr. Chops, the dwarf, "had a kind of a everlasting grudge agin the Public: which is a thing you may notice in many phenomenons that get their living out of it." Few have equaled him in spilling out paragraphs, written apparently without effort, which are more irresistible in their cadences and antitheses than that famous introductory passage in *A Tale of Two Cities,* "It was the best of times, it was the worst of times, it was the age of wisdom, it was the age of foolishness, it was the epoch of belief, it was the epoch of incredulity," etc., etc.

The feat Mr. Williams performs is also remarkable. He brings both Dickens and his works to life with enchanting and astonishing skill. Although he might have selected greater scenes, the ones he has chosen are more than satisfactory and could not be better done.

February 23, 1952

The Bane of the Bassinet

꒜꒜꒜꒜꒜꒜꒜꒜꒜꒜꒜꒜꒜꒜꒜꒜꒜꒜꒜꒜꒜꒜꒜꒜꒜꒜꒜꒜꒜

Marijuana of the Nursery

COMIC BOOKS, alas, like death and taxes, are very much with us. And, to my way of thinking, they are equally unfunny. Why they are called comics, when people who read them—young and old—almost always look like undertakers, eludes me. But we'll let that pass. Just as most of us as parents have had to let comics pass into our homes—against our wills, against our wishes, against our better judgment.

I love comedians, the highest and the lowest. I love cartoons, too. My allergy to comic books, however, is complete, utter, absolute. I know there are bad comics, and I presume there are good comics. I have read a few of both—under protest. But I regret them both. I deplore them. And, to continue the understatement, I abhor them. So far as I am concerned, they might just as well be written in a foreign language for which no dictionary has ever been published. I wish they had been.

Let me quickly admit that I am low enough, and sometimes defeated enough, as a parent, to make use of comic books. I mean in desperate moments when, of a rainy Sunday morning or afternoon, I want peace in the home. Or when I am traveling with my two sons on a train and need to subdue them. Then

—yes, I'll confess it—then I do resort to comics. Without shame. Without conscience.

On such occasions I don't so much distribute comics as I administer them to my sons. Much as a barkeep would pour out a Mickey Finn. Or a doctor employ a hypodermic. As knockout drops for unruly children, as sedatives and Maxim silencers, comics do have their undeniable uses. This much I'll concede, gratefully.

I'll also grant that so long as other people's children read comics we have scant hope, and perhaps less right, to keep our own from doing so. It would be unfair for us to deny to our children what is now a group experience and, when they have grown up, will have become a group memory of their generation.

If I hate comic books, I have my reasons. I know that, as part of a healthy diet, everyone needs a certain amount of trash. Each generation has always found its own trash. I doubt if our grandfathers were harmed by the dime novels about Kit Carson, Jesse James, etc., on which they fed. I doubt, too, if Little Nemo, Mutt and Jeff, Foxy Grandpa, Buster Brown, or the Katzenjammer Kids did serious damage to those of my vintage when we read them once a week.

Give me Henty, *The Rover Boys, The Motor Boys,* or *Tom Swift on the Mississippi,* or any books written in words for those who can read, any day in preference to the comic books. The comic books, however, as they are nowadays perpetually on tap, seem to me to be, not only trash, but the lowest, most despicable and most harmful form of trash. As a rule, their word selection is as wretched as their drawing, or the paper on which they are printed. They are designed for readers who are too lazy to read, and increase both their unwillingness and inability to do so.

I won't and can't deny that comic books fascinate the young as, in terms of pigs, rabbits, rodents, morons, and supermen, they tell their illustrated stories. But, as a writer, I resent the way in which they get along with the poorest kind of writing. I hate their lack of both style and ethics. I hate their appeal to illiteracy and their bad grammar. I loathe their tiresome toughness, their cheap thrills, their imbecilic laughter.

I despise them for making only the story count and not the HOW of its telling. I detest them, in spite of their alleged thrills and gags, because they have no subtlety, and certainly no beauty. Their power of seduction, I believe, lies in the fact that they make everything too easy. They substitute bad drawing for good description. They reduce the wonders of the language to crude monosyllables, and narratives to no more than printed motion pictures.

What riles me when I see my children absorbed by the comics is my awareness of what they are not reading, and could be reading. In other words, of the more genuine and deeper pleasures that they could be having.

To compare Bugs Bunny or Donald Duck with *The Jungle Book* or even *The Travels of Babar;* to set Wanda, the Wonder Woman against *Alice in Wonderland,* Batman and Robin, Dick Tracy, and Gene Autry against *Treasure Island,* Li'l Abner against *Huck Finn* or *Tom Sawyer,* or Superman and Captain Marvel against Jules Verne or *Gulliver's Travels,* is to realize that, between the modern cave-drawing (which a comic book is) and a real book, there is—to put it mildly—a difference. A tragic difference, which is hard on the young, and may be harder on the future.

Anatole France once described even the best books as being "the opium of the Occident." Well, most comic books, as I see them, are the marijuana of the nursery; the bane of the bassinet; the horror of the home; the curse of the kids; and a threat to the future. They offer final and melancholy proof that, even among the young, the mind is the most unused muscle in the United States.

I don't care how popular comic books are with the young or, worse still, with the old. They seem to me to be sad proofs of arrested undevelopment. Time in the modern world is no longer something to be wasted. The moment has overtaken us, whether we like it or not, and most of us do not, when as a people we must grow up. In order to grow up, we must put behind us that fear of the best and that lust for the mediocre which most Americans cultivate.

March 20, 1948

THE MURDER most foul, strange, and unnatural committed on Macbeth *by turning it into a Comic Book, and some of the widespread misconceptions represented by such a deed.*

Knock, Knock, Knock!

I DO NOT happen to know John W. Griffin, but on the basis of a form letter he has written as president of Seaboard Publishers, Inc., I am persuaded he is an utterly sincere man. Seaboard Publishers are manufacturers of comic books, and Mr. Griffin is a person who approaches this sometimes unadmired industry as a realist and a reformer.

The little number he has sent my way as a trial balloon is, of all things, a comic-book edition of William Shakespeare's *Macbeth.* * Like many another so-called comic, this cartoon version of Shakespeare's tragedy is not meant to be funny. Yet it must be catalogued as a comic if for no other reason than that it employs the methods and format of those polychrome publications which are usually so classified. The result, to put it mildly, is a production of *Macbeth* quite different from any to which the play has been exposed in its long and varied history.

* *Macbeth*, by William Shakespeare. No. 6 in a Treasury of Celebrated Literature; Stories by Famous Authors Illustrated. Adapted as a Comic Book by Dana E. Dutch, illustrated by H. C. Kiefer, lettered by H. G. Ferguson. New York: Seaboard Publishers, Inc. 30 pp. 10¢.

· 145 ·

The Bane of the Bassinet

Before coming to this new *Macbeth* it seems only fair to let Mr. Griffin explain the service he thought he was performing by undertaking it. Did I say Mr. Griffin was at once a realist and a reformer? Let me make both points clear. Mr. Griffin reminds us that over forty million comic magazines are sold each month and nearly two hundred titles are regularly published, ranging, as he puts it, "all the way from the completely harmless to some which are highly objectionable." Furthermore, he says, and he ought to know, though it depresses me to share this knowledge, that such books "are about the only reading matter purchased by many children and an increasing number of adults."

"The comics are here—and here to stay," states he, as if any parent would challenge him. Mr. Griffin's lofty aim, therefore, is to make the best of a bad situation by providing "as fine a 'comic book' as it is possible to produce." The first step toward doing this, he believes, is to derive comics from authors who have "real cultural worth." Hence this *Macbeth*.

In reading this *Macbeth* Mr. Griffin urges us to keep in mind the audience for which it has been written: "first, the adult who has read few, if any, solid, substantial books; and, second, the high-school student who is seeking an auxiliary aid to his high-school work." Mr. Griffin is well aware that his *Macbeth* is not "an effective substitute for the original." His hope is, however, that it will serve as a sufficient indication of "this great drama's . . . breadth and power" to lead perhaps some readers to Shakespeare himself.

A slight but not unwarranted uncertainty seems to have Mr. Griffin in its grip. At one moment he confidently risks the guess that his comic-book *Macbeth* will be recognized "as an interesting experiment in literature." At the next he invites a candid opinion as to whether it "will serve any good purpose" and if other such Shakespearean comics should be released.

My last desire is to be impolite to so well-meaning a fellow as Mr. Griffin. But, since he has asked for candor, candor he shall have. Mr. Griffin, it seems to me, is about as wrong-headed in his pursuit of what is right as it is possible to be. He is not lonely in his errors. Like many another, he appears to have been misguided by his good intentions. He and his benevolent associates at Seaboard have, in my opinion, succumbed in the name of literacy, culture, or what you will, to a list of fallacies based upon misconceptions so widespread that they merit discussion.

In fairness to Mr. Griffin and his firm it must be admitted that they are not the first offenders in a misleading practice. They are merely followers of a false tradition. There have been so-called classic comics for some time; comics masquerading as educational which have sought to turn such defenseless novels as *The Three Musketeers, Ivanhoe, Don Quixote, Moby Dick, The Last of the Mohicans,* or *Huckleberry Finn* into blood brothers of Li'l Abner, the Lone Ranger, Captain Marvel, Gandy and Sourpuss, Flash Gordon, and Mandrake the Magician.

These have been bad enough. That they were designed to do good I am willing to concede, but that they have succeeded in doing good I cannot bring myself to believe. They have had no other choice than to make molehills out of mountains and mudpies out of classics. For the misapprehension underlying them is the same one which lies behind this comic-book *Macbeth.*

In its fashion they have confused one medium with another. They have offered chromos with captions, asking their readers

The Bane of the Bassinet

to accept them as masterpieces. They have peddled what is not even a substitute and pretended it was an equivalent. They have become victims of the false notion that those who might just as well be illiterates can be made lovers of literature by reading an aggressively unliterary version of a classic. Moreover, they have deceived American youngsters by inducing them to accept as truth an untruth apparently subscribed to by many of their elders; namely, that to know the story an author tells is not only to know the author and his book but to have shared in the pleasures and distinctions of his writing.

Gross as the vulgarities of these earlier classic comics have been, their offenses somehow seem mild compared to those which this cartoon *Macbeth* is bound to commit. To rob a prose writer of his prose can be, depending upon the writer in question, either petty or grand larceny. But to rob a sublime poet of his poetry and a supreme dramatist of the form at which he excelled is mayhem plus murder in the first degree.

Much as I love them, I have to confess that when Charles and Mary Lamb collaborated on their *Tales from Shakespeare* they set a bad example. Without their realizing it, they were opening wide the sluice-gates for future generations of lesser synopses manufacturers and addicts. Their hope was to earn a needed penny and to help a publisher friend. Elia had no illusions about the results. "I think it will be popular among the little people," wrote he. He was right. It was. Yet I doubt if he foresaw how numerous the "little people" were even then, how their numbers would multiply down the decades, and how abundantly they would, in our times, include alleged grown-ups in their ranks.

What Elia as the Bard's first nursery-popularizer would say of this new Mandrake-the-Magician adaptation of *Macbeth*, I tremble to think. My conviction is that he would be outraged by every picture and every caption on every page of the whole melancholy proceedings. For this very reason he would, no doubt, blush Kremlin-red because of his own share in the *Tales* which, though the work of angels compared to the witches' brew of this present-day *Macbeth*, inadvertently prepared the way for it.

Although I have sat through many revivals of the tragedy, some of which have claimed their scattered excellences but most of which have been inadequate, I never expected to be confronted with a production as wretched as the one these well-meaning publishers have made in the hope of tempting young people of all ages to Shakespeare. The plot is there, faithfully followed yet whittled down to its bare essentials, with all its excitements gone, its tensions lost, its scenes denied the suspense and terror of their building.

Snippets of the original dialogue are here and there to be encountered, running true for a sentence or two, then suddenly being cut, colloquialized, or altered so that the song of the speeches is muted, their sense abandoned, their grandeur destroyed. What once soared no longer has wings to flutter. It is earth-bound throughout, a travesty of itself, and by its very solemnity almost a travesty of the ineptitudes of comics, too. Although the tale is murderous and gory, it never rises beyond cheap horror into true tragedy or even superb melodrama.

If the language deflates the drama, so do the drawings. The colors are hideous. The human figures are empty parodies of what the parts demand. The witches are Dogpatch ugly without being Dogpatch funny, and the medieval backgrounds are scenery of so outmoded a kind that even Edwin Forrest would have refused to play before them. The mystery of darkness, the supernatural terrors of the heath, the agonies of introspection, the drive and depth of the drama, indeed its greatness which in the theatre or in the library is its excuse and glory— all these are pitifully missing. What is left is not a tragedy. It is trashcan stuff.

Certainly no one can be hurt by knowing the story of *Macbeth*. Yet just as surely no one can pretend to know *Macbeth* who knows only its story and has encountered it in such a form. This is the glaring delusion to which Mr. Griffin and his confreres have surrendered in the interest of what they apparently believe, and would have their readers young and old believe, is "culture."

A final comment on their comic-book *Macbeth* is the note on its garish cover, "Adapted from the Original Text for EASY and ENJOYABLE Reading!" Perhaps one of the reasons so many people in this country have been left uneducated by their educations is that everything is made too easy for them. To be understood and enjoyed, the great works, which are the products of strong feeling or hard thinking, require similar responses. Giving of the best, they demand the best, to be appreciated. They cannot be vulgarized without being violated. Theirs is an integrity no less than a beauty which should summon from us an integrity of our own.

The difference between Shakespeare's *Macbeth* and Seaboard's is too great for comfort and almost great enough for nausea. Give me Li'l Abner and Daisy Mae any day. Please, Mr. Griffin and your high-minded associates, stop trying to create "culture" by deriving comics from authors who, in your unhappy phrase, "have real cultural worth." Let us have comics which are comics, not classics which have ceased to be classics but have dwindled into comics. Leave the masterpieces un-raped. Don't fool yourselves and us by pretending that what they are not is what you would have us believe they are. Don't be guilty of trying to make everything easy. Greatness in literature is bound to present its challenges if not its difficulties. This is one of the reasons for its being enjoyable.

July 29, 1950

A ONCE-LOYAL member of the Walt
Disney Club finds, to his sorrow, that he
is now happiest when he stays away from
Mr. Disney's full-length animated films.

ᴬᴬᴬᴬᴬᴬᴬᴬᴬᴬᴬᴬᴬᴬᴬᴬᴬᴬᴬᴬᴬᴬᴬᴬᴬᴬᴬᴬᴬᴬᴬᴬᴬᴬᴬᴬᴬ

Recessional

AS SURELY as mountain ranges climb to peaks, careers rise to their summits. It is hard to pick out the highest of these at the moment of its being reached. Even in retrospect specifying them can be a hazardous business. I feel fairly safe, however, in contending that June 22 and 23, 1938, cannot have been unpleasant days for Walt Disney. Superman though he is, he would not be human had they not been for him days when the earth was very much in tune.

On the first of these June days, along with Thomas Mann, Lord Tweedsmuir, and Serge Koussevitzky, Mr. Disney received an honorary degree at Yale. He must have been gratified by President Seymour's citation, which described him as the "creator of a new language of art, who has brought the joy of deep laughter to millions and, by touching the heart of humanity without distinction of race, has served as an ambassador of international good will." He must have been even more delighted when William Lyon Phelps presented him to Dr. Seymour as the man who "labored like a mountain and brought forth a mouse, with which he conquered the whole world."

The very next day, and once again in Lord Tweedsmuir's

company, Mr. Disney received the same kind of tribute at Harvard. There he was characterized by President Conant as "a magician who has created a modern dwelling for the muses; his hand controls a multitude of elfish animals who charm all humans by their mirth."

These two days of academic honors could not have displeased even so unacademic a figure as Mr. Disney. Although neither university could pretend to have discovered him, both had put upon him the official seal of recognition which Mr. Disney's admirers everywhere had long since been convinced was his due. There were, to be sure, big Disney years ahead. *Pinocchio, Bambi, Dumbo,* and *Fantasia* were still in the offing. But by the spring of 1938 the tide of Mr. Disney's reputation, if not at the flood, was approaching it.

He had created a new world by animating an old one. His imagination was as universally recognized as the rough-and-tumble of his humor was appreciated. He did not have to hire actors. He merely had to draw them, and they in turn drew huge audiences and countless devotees. Unlike Darwin, who had contented himself with writing about the origin of the species, Mr. Disney had originated a species of his own. He was an unnatural rather than a natural historian. The animal kingdom over which he ruled supreme was an inspired cross between Aesop and the comic strips. The Ark never housed such high-spirited and rambunctious creatures as his. Had it done so, it might have been a happier ship but its chances of keeping afloat for those forty days and nights would have been lessened.

Wherever there were motion-picture theatres Mickey Mouse had by 1938 proved a rodent with the beckoning abilities of the Pied Piper. Mr. Disney's Donald was a duck which had by then flown much farther than Ibsen's wild one. His Three Little Pigs had reached markets undreamed of by the Cudahys, the Swifts, and the Armours. No house was safe against the huffing and puffing of his Big Bad Wolf. His Pluto was a pet to millions unable to identify Sirius, that oldest dog star.

Moreover, this same 1938 which had brought academic honors to Mr. Disney was a year that had been made at once the more agreeable and memorable by the release of his *Snow White and the Seven Dwarfs*. Plainly his career had taken on a new dimension. It was as if a master of the short story had triumphed as a novelist. Regardless of the reservations some of us may have had about the vacuity of Mr. Disney's Snow White, the frightening wickedness of his Witch, or the utter blankness of his Prince Charming, his birds and squirrels (which used their tails like Fuller brushes) and, above all, his Seven Dwarfs had captured everyone's heart and imagination. Mr. Disney's conquest of adults was as thoroughgoing as his victory over universities and youth.

I could not help thinking back to the Disney of 1938 and those subsequent peak years when recently I sat before his *Cinderella*.* I could not help thinking back to the enthusiasm which I had then felt for his work and which, little by little, has chilled into indifference.

There are enchanting moments in his new film; moments of pure Disneyana; moments when such humanized animals as Gus-Gus, the thick-headed mouse, Lucifer, the swollen but

---

* *Cinderella*, a Walt Disney feature-length cartoon based on the Charles Perrault fairy tale. Story by William Peed, Ted Sears, Erdman Penner, Winston Hibler, and Harry Reeves. Directed by Wilfred Jackson, Hamilton Luske, and Clyde Geronimi. Musical direction by Oliver Wallace and Paul Smith, with songs by Mack David, Jerry Levingstone, and Al Hoffman. Production supervised by Ben Sharpsteen. Distributed by RKO Radio Pictures.

sinister cat, or Bruno, the Plutoish canine, cast the old Disney spell. There is a fine sequence, too, in which a shower of soap bubbles makes the screen magical. There is the even more mesmerizing interlude in which, while tiny twinkling stars spout from the Fairy Godmother's wand, the pumpkin is transformed into a coach and Cinderella's friendly mice into horses. As "Bibbidi-Bobbidi Boo" was being sung, I must admit I rejoiced in something of that same sense of release which all of us used to experience when we responded to "Who's Afraid of the Big Bad Wolf?" "Whistle While You Work," "Heigh-Ho," "Hi Diddle Dee Dee," or "When I See an Elephant Fly."

Yet, trusting the estate of Parson Weems will not sue me for plagiarism, I cannot tell a lie. Then and there my enjoyment of *Cinderella* came to a precipitous end. The wonder I had first felt in the presence of Mr. Disney's work was absent; the original delight had fled. Misgivings pushed satisfaction aside; tedium replaced surrender. Ennui, and not a minor ennui either, had set in. Save for the exceptions noted above, it plagued me during most of the performance.

It is easy for me to find rational explanations for my sorry state. *Cinderella* may be a young-girl's dream or an old-wives' tale but, as a story, it is scarcely an older man's delight. I remember resisting it as a boy and finding it yawnful even when jam-stealing was my notion of the ultimate sin. The reasons for my disrelish of Mr. Disney's treatment of it did not stop there. Since the film left my attention unemployed, it gave me time to explore them.

For example, there are the technical problems with which this drudge-into-princess fable confronts Mr. Disney. Mr. Disney has never done his best work in the human zoo. His creatures, fur- or feather-bearing, have been his matchless creations —these and such of his masterpieces of grotesquerie as the Seven Dwarfs. His heroes and heroines, in particular, have eluded him. They have tended to be bloodless transparencies cursed with wafer faces. They have not been individuals; they have been vacant lots. His wicked mortals, although more successful, have likewise left something to be desired. As a rule, they have been no more than funny-paper figures which have satisfied the kiddie-car rather than the carriage trade.

Mr. Disney is, of course, free to populate his *Cinderella* with as many animals as he pleases, and with these he scores his expected success. He is, however, also committed to representing an unusually large number of human characters. The story being the story it is, he cannot turn his back on Cinderella, her stepmother, the two stepsisters, the Fairy Godmother, the Prince, the King, and his emissary (call him chamberlain, Grand Duke, or what you will). In other words, this means that Mr. Disney starts with eight strikes against him.

There is yet another rational cause for having lost one's first enthusiasm for Mr. Disney's products. No one can minimize his contribution, question his invention, or challenge his imagination. Yet Mr. Disney's taste has always been an uncertain factor. Each passing year has made this clearer and clearer. Certainly his mixture of drawn and real people in such a film as *The Three Caballeros* was one of the most unfortunate experiments since Prohibition.

Then, for a gay and witty fellow, Mr. Disney's calendar has, in his longer efforts, included an unconscionable number of St. Valentine's days. He can swig syrup apparently under the impression that he is drinking coffee. His is a wavering genius. At one moment he can function brilliantly and unmistakably as an artist; at the next he can sink below the standards of a greeting-card designer. *Cinderella* abounds in such unfortunate lapses. Consider Mr. Disney's treatment of the King's palace. Most of us have long ago outlived our infatuation for Maxfield Parrish. One might guess from the tapering towers of Mr. Disney's castle that he was just beginning his. As a matter of cold and ugly fact, he manages to out-Parrish Parrish in conjuring sentimental dreamlands, royal residences built on clouds, and wedding-cake versions of Mont St. Michel.

Mr. Disney's Cinderella offers difficulties of her own. She is a blank-faced blonde, armed Al Capp-a-pie with the allurements of Daisy Mae. Although she may have to do the dirty work around her stepmother's home, she remains miraculously undirtied. There is nothing of the ill-used waif about her. Plainly she eats well, is delighted with her looks, and from the outset is bound to win the Prince. She is, in short, a smug little number with a mind as empty as a diary received on Christmas morning. Her animal magnetism is infinite. This is proved by her being attended by enough adoring mice and birds to try the patience of St. Francis.

What bothers me with *Cinderella*, however, is not this or that reservation I happen to have about it. What I cannot explain to my own satisfaction is why over the years Mr. Disney's films, in spite of their persisting virtues, have ceased to give me pleasure. They continue to grow in their technical excellences. They continue to boast their first ingenuities. They continue to demonstrate in incident after incident that the man responsible for them is a genius of sorts. Yet, where I once hastened to see them, I must confess I now am inclined to avoid them.

Is it because I have grown older? Is it because repetition is

bound to have robbed his work of its novelty? Is it because Mr.
Disney at present fails me or I fail him? Or is it because of the
very nature of the medium at which he excels? Is it because
this is a medium that, in spite of the courage and success of his
attempts to alter and enlarge it, is nonetheless limited?

I cannot say. I do not know. I know only that my infidelity
disturbs me. I cannot deny it. It exists. As the Bard of Brattle
Street would have put it, it is real, it is earnest. It is more, I
suspect, than the product of capriciousness. Overexposure has,
doubtless, played its part. Even so, such ingratitude shames
me. Yet there it is—stubborn, insistent, and genuine. The paradox is that, though formerly I would have sworn mine was a
life membership in that huge fraternity known as the Disney
Club, I no longer find myself capable even of a sustaining membership. I cannot quite bring myself to end an association, once
so pleasant, by resigning. I have, however, discovered the ad-
vantages of a nonresident status. To my surprise I have come
to realize I am happiest, and most loyal, when I stay away
from meetings.

June 3, 1950

Dramatis Personae

THE TONIC effects of Italy, and the untraditional way in which a supposedly happy Tennessee Williams has responded to them both as novelist and dramatist.

~~~~~~

Saying It with Flowers

FROM WHAT he had said to interviewers and from what my confreres had said about *The Rose Tattoo,** my impression was that Tennessee Williams had of late stumbled upon happiness. No longer, I was led to believe, was Mr. Williams a spokesman for frustration. No longer was he rewriting with deepening variations the theme of Southern sadness and despair which had served him, and served him well, in *The Glass Menagerie* and *A Streetcar Named Desire.* I gathered that a new Mr. Williams had appeared; a positive fellow who had put negation behind him; a man who had brushed the Spanish moss from his thinking, turned his back on meanness and decay, and walked out of the shadows into the bright light of noon.

Mr. Williams's explanation of his changed mood was not an unusual one. In a word, it was Italy. And Italy, seen at the

* *The Rose Tattoo,* by Tennessee Williams. Directed by Daniel Mann. Settings by Boris Aronson. Costumes by Rose Bogdanoff. Incidental music by David Diamond. Presented by Cheryl Crawford. With a cast including Maureen Stapleton, Eli Wallach, Phyllis Love, Don Murray, Robert Carricart, etc. At the Martin Beck Theatre, New York City. Opened February 3, 1951.

right seasons under the right circumstances, has over the centuries lifted the spirits of millions of travelers. Playwrights no less than poets, novelists, and ordinary trippers have responded to the curative powers of its sunshine and the sunnier aspects of its people. It was Italy, after all, which healed Goethe. It brought him "a new youth," restored him "to the enjoyment of life," and persuaded him to count the day he entered Rome as "a second birthday, a true regeneration." Even Ibsen so thawed under Italian skies that, more than gurgling about all that was "beautiful, wonderful, magical" in Rome, he boasted he felt there "an extraordinary capacity for work and the strength of a giantkiller."

No wonder then that Mr. Williams, who wrote *The Rose Tattoo* during his recent Roman holiday, was reported to have reacted to the stimulations of Italy in what seemed to be the traditional way. "I have felt more hopeful about human nature as a result of being exposed to the Italians," said he to a reporter. He also confessed that not only was his new play directly inspired by "the vitality, humanity, and love of life expressed by the Italian people" but that he himself had felt "much happier in the last two or three years than ever in my life."

Remembering these exuberant statements and recollecting my fellow reviewers' assertions to the effect that Mr. Williams had found a new formula for his plays and was in a cheerful frame of mind, I naturally approached *The Rose Tattoo* expecting it to be gayer than *The Gondoliers*, and more persuasive than Pippa ever was in proving that "all's right with the world." My fear is, however, that I was anticipating the impossible. I was expecting the mourning dove to borrow the bluebird's song and the pond lily to turn into the hollyhock. I had apparently forgotten all things are relative and that what is hailed as optimism in Mr. Williams might be described as pessimism (or at least an odd manifestation of faith and joy) in almost everyone else.

I do not doubt that Mr. Williams found delight in his Italian sojourn or that he was revitalized by it. Certainly his former languor has been replaced by a fresh energy in the dialogue he has written for *The Rose Tattoo*. Yet, on the basis of the subjects he chose to deal with in the novel and the play he wrote in Italy, it would seem to me that he must have been drinking vinegar under the impression that it was chianti.

I do not, for example, see how anyone could read *The Roman Spring of Mrs. Stone* without realizing that in addition to being a less than indifferent work of fiction it is a resolutely disagreeable study of decadence and degeneracy. If its picture of how a widowed and retired actress turns from one gigolo who is bad to another who is worse is a reflection of Mr. Williams's happiness, then *Crime and Punishment* belongs in the Little Colonel Series and *Mlle. de Maupin* takes its place among the Freddy Books.

Permit me to turn, however, from Mr. Williams's novel, as I am only too glad to do, and come back to *The Rose Tattoo*, that new play of his in which supposedly he has written a sequel to *Peace of Mind* and *Words to Live By*. In it, though his scene is once again the South, Mr. Williams indicates the broadening effects of travel by choosing as his Southerners this time Sicilians who live in a village on the Gulf somewhere between New Orleans and Mobile.

Before coming to his treatment of these warm-blooded people, it may be worth while to delve into his theme, searching there for indications of the fine and original affirmations with which the now-hopeful Mr. Williams has been credited. His heroine is the widow of a truck-driver who is obsessed by the memory of her husband. He has been killed in an accident while delivering narcotics under a load of bananas. For three years (here is one of Mr. Williams's Pollyanna touches) his widow lives a fanatic's life, closeted in her shack with the urn containing her husband's ashes.

She refuses, at first, to let her daughter marry the young sailor who is in love with her. Her memory of the love she has had is all that keeps the widow alive. In spite of the whispers of local gossips, she believes her husband, who had a rose tattooed on his chest, was faithful to her. It is only when she discovers by means of the telephone, in one of the most awkward scenes I can remember, that a professional woman not only shared her husband but sports an identical rose tattoo that the widow is willing to consider the new truck-driver who has suddenly stopped at her door. Though he has the face of a clown and the body of her husband, it turns out that this new arrival also has a rose tattoo on his chest. Thereupon the widow smashes the urn, breaks with the past by letting the breezes dispose of her husband's ashes, and gives herself to the new truck-driver.

Do not ask me to describe the meaning of all the roses, real or imaginary, with which several of Mr. Williams's characters are tattooed. Let me only confess that not since the Houses of York and Lancaster feuded long and publicly have roses been used more lavishly than by Mr. Williams. To Gertrude Stein a rose was a rose was a rose. But to Mr. Williams roses are mystical signs, proofs of passion, symbols of devotion, and buds no less than thorns in the flesh. Mr. Williams's roses, moreover, are not real blooms. Instead, they are dramatically the equivalents of so many cheap paper flowers used to fancy up a lot of downright foolishness.

Just how this story of a half-crazed widow's willingness to marry again can be taken as evidence of a smiling and constructive attitude on Mr. Williams's part also eludes me. Widows, after all, have remarried before and will remarry again. Certainly it is no discovery to realize that life must be continued and must renew itself. Yet one thing I neither can nor wish to deny. Ridiculous as his plot may be, such is the magic of Mr. Williams's dialogue, such is the beauty with which he writes this scene or that, and so admirable are the acting and staging of his new play that *The Rose Tattoo* casts a spell while it is being seen. I know it did on me.

Even when I did not believe in it, even when it seemed operatic in its absurdities, I found myself listening. Its speech is properly volcanic for characters whose ancestors were born near Etna. Its intentional humor is colorful and pungent. Regardless, too, of how bogus its big table-thumping climaxes may be, Mr. Williams's writing of them has its hypnotic qualities.

Mr. Williams is a tantalizing dramatist. Although his gifts are many and unmistakable, his shortcomings are almost as manifest. His intuitive understanding of his characters is remarkable. So is the sensitivity with which he can develop such a scene as the fine one of the courtship of the sailor and the daughter. But he is a wasteful writer who has no disciplined sense of form or structure. His innumerable villagers, for example, never quite succeed in serving as the Chorus they were plainly meant to be. Mr. Williams is at his best when he writes simply and directly as an emotionalist and at his weakest when he is pretentious and carries symbolism to exasperating lengths. He sees, he hears, he feels, but he does not appear to think.

Perhaps this is why, notwithstanding its rare qualities, *The Rose Tattoo* does not bear thinking about. It collapses under analysis.

What does bear thinking about, and retains its savor long after the curtain is down, is the brilliant manner in which Daniel Mann has staged *The Rose Tattoo,* the excellence of Boris Aronson's setting, and the superior skill with which its principal parts are acted. Phyllis Love and Don Murray play the daughter and the sailor with a glistening tenderness and innocence. As the truck-driver, who is really Mr. Williams's ever-recurrent character the Gentleman Caller, this time with an Italian accent, Eli Wallach is wonderfully buoyant and naive. But the evening's outstanding performance is Maureen Stapleton's playing of the widow. She has a driving intensity. Hers is a passion that is all flame. Obviously she so believes in the part that she comes near to convincing even those of us who do not that it is all she thinks it is.

This leads me back to Mr. Williams's play which, in spite of its virtues, seems to me unworthy of all the skill which he and his associates have squandered upon it. It is empty at its center. False, too. If the ugly truth must out, it comes perilously close to being silly.

March 10, 1951

THE MISFORTUNE of having a career start off at its apex, and the absurdity of treating a writer when he writes badly as if he had done so on purpose.

Mr. Odets's Return

NO ONE interested in the theatre can fail to take an almost personal satisfaction in the success which, with *The Country Girl,** has again come to Clifford Odets, and come because of his having deserved it. Success is a strange matter, as Mr. Odets is in a better position to know than most. He achieved it early—and with a bang. He was twenty-nine when *Waiting for Lefty* exploded like a bomb behind New York's footlights and when in *Awake and Sing* he wrote one of the richest, warmest, and most probing dramas an American has written in our time. This was in 1935, a year which theatrically must be described as an Odets year. During this same season *Till the Day I Die* and *Paradise Lost* also reached production, and playgoers experienced the exhilaration which comes from realizing that a new, fine, and magnificently vigorous talent has emerged.

* *The Country Girl*, by Clifford Odets. Staged by Mr. Odets. Settings by Boris Aronson. Costumes by Anna Hill Johnstone. Dwight Deere Wiman presents the Strasberg and Odets Production. With Paul Kelly, Uta Hagen, Steven Hill, Peter Kass, Louis Veda Quince, Joseph Sullivan, Phyllis Love, and Tony Albert. At the Lyceum Theatre, New York City. Opened November 10, 1950.

Mr. Odets's career can be said to have got off to a poor start if for no other reason than that it started off too well. It did not work up to a climax; it began with one. It commenced, so to speak, with the fifth act—a process which, however heady and exciting, is not in accordance with the safer canons of dramatic practice. The challenge with which it confronted Mr. Odets was cruel. In the years following his initial triumph he was bound to be penalized by his own achievement. He had to live up to himself, and so great was the hope his admirers had invested in him that this amounted to his having to live down his own reputation. This is why Mr. Odets must know, as few do, how bitter the sweet fruits of success can become.

Trigorin in *The Sea Gull* was aware of one of the most poignant aspects of literary endeavor: the realization that what one has written is neither what one wanted to write nor so good as what others have written on the same subject. When a novel of his was printed, Trigorin said the public read it but always with the comment, "Yes, charming, clever. Charming but nothing like Tolstoy. A very fine thing, but Turgenev's *Fathers and Sons* is finer." Trigorin's lament was that, when he was dead, they would be saying at his grave, "Here lies Trigorin, a delightful writer but not so good as Turgenev."

Since 1935 Mr. Odets has suffered a sadder fate than Trigorin's. Instead of being compared unfavorably with his betters, he has been compared unfavorably with Odets. From *Golden Boy* (1937) to *The Big Knife* (1949) there was a marked falling off. Slow as it was, it was steady and disheartening. Although proofs of the old Odets magic were to be found in such new plays as *Rocket to the Moon, Night Music,* and *Clash by Night,* these proofs gradually became rarer and rarer.

Indeed, there were many of us who, two seasons back when

we saw *The Big Knife*, became truly concerned about Mr. Odets. It seemed as if his talent had slowly dried up. He was scolded, of course, as if the fault were his. When writers who have pleased us by writing well disappoint us by writing badly, their fate is to be treated as if they wrote badly on purpose. One of the more ridiculous aspects of criticism is the regularity with which it finds people who cannot write telling people who can that they should have written better. Unquestionably they are writing as well as their gifts permit them to *at that time*. All of us are apt to forget that authors cannot subpoena genius and that a writer's talent may leave him as unpredictably as a singer's voice. This is what appears to have happened to Mr. Odets. This is why, too, it is agreeable to be able to report that in *The Country Girl* the stream which had thinned to a trickle is flowing once more.

Although *The Country Girl* is not Mr. Odets's best play, it has some of his best writing in it. Moreover, it discloses a new and unexpected Odets. This in itself is reassuring and welcome. Mr. Odets has usually been associated with dramas of social significance if not of social protest. His favorite theme song, sung in anger or with enormous vitality, has been "Awake and sing, ye that dwell in the dust." His characters have shared "a fundamental activity: a struggle for life amidst petty conditions." His explanation of their personal frailties used to be the over-simple one that they were victims of The System.

It is interesting to see in *The Country Girl* that Mr. Odets can write from affection with the same intensity and insight with which he first wrote from indignation. This time he is making no plea, addressing no mass meeting, and leaving The System not only unblamed but unmentioned. The theatre, which he loves as warmly as he hates Hollywood, is his background, and its people are his concern. He is telling the story, a messageless one, of how a devoted wife struggles to keep her actor-husband sober so that he can make a comeback in the leading part a trusting producer is convinced he can play. The director falls in love with the wife after having at first misunderstood her. At the end, however, hers is Candida's choice of the man who has the greater need of her because he is the weaker.

Plainly such a theme in such a setting is neither new nor earth-shaking. As Sidney Howard pointed out long ago, the age and service-stripes of a story have little to do with eligibility. The point is that Mr. Odets makes the story his own. He gives it the benefit of his high-voltage feeling and phrasing. He allows us to see far beneath the surface of his characters into what is the mainspring of their frustrations or their actions. With skill and subtlety he misleads us at the outset into accepting as true the lies the actor has told about his wife in order to excuse his own weaknesses. Then, little by little, Mr. Odets enables us to see her as she is. His scenes race forward with the drive of his earliest works. His gift for deriving tension from small things is as effective as it used to be in developing large climaxes.

The originality which sharpens his writing is equally present in his direction. The sense of hard-pressed poverty, of abandoned hope, and of squandered talents which he establishes is admirably visualized in Boris Aronson's sordid dressing-room and pathetic boarding-house backgrounds. As the maligned yet faithful wife, Uta Hagen plays quietly, knowingly, without any cheap bids for sympathy, but with an indomitable inner strength. Although personally I prefer Paul Kelly in such a tough, tight-lipped role as the General in *Command Decision*, I cannot deny his excellence as the alcoholic actor. He captures the irresolution, amiability, and pathetic self-deception of this man who has ruined his career and his wife's life. Steven Hill is no less successful as the dynamic director, dictatorial in his ways, and accustomed to believing himself and having others believe in his own snap judgments regardless of how wrong they may be.

When *The Big Knife* opened two seasons ago, I was forced to confess, "Few scripts have made me more uncomfortably aware of the inner despair of the authors; few have left me more apprehensive about their writers' immediate future." *The Country Girl* makes such apprehension groundless. After a stormy and troubled period Mr. Odets has refound himself and his talent. This should mean a great deal to our theatre which stands desperately in need of all that is energizing and distinguished in his gifts.

December 9, 1950

*AN OLD Communist finds himself the
victim of the order he helped create and,
though he knows the truth, dies telling
the lie that his imprisoned mind makes
natural to him.*

The Iron Transparency

"**I** SERVED the Communist Party for seven years—the
same length of time as Jacob tended Laban's sheep to win
Rachel his daughter. When the time was up, the bride was led
into his dark tent; only the next morning did he discover that
his ardors had been spent not on the lovely Rachel but on the
ugly Leah. I wonder whether he ever recovered from the shock
of having slept with an illusion. I wonder whether afterwards
he believed that he had ever believed in it."

In this manner, and a vivid manner it is, Arthur Koestler
concludes his contribution to *The God That Failed.* Surely
most readers interested in following the inner workings of the
Communist Party and learning the extent to which it degrades
and humiliates artists and thinkers must by now have read this
important anthology. In it such writers as Ignazio Silone, Richard Wright, André Gide, Louis Fischer, Stephen Spender, and
Mr. Koestler have frankly analyzed the misplaced idealism
which in the Twenties or Thirties persuaded them to become
Party members. With the utmost candor they have described
their disillusioning experiences and given the reasons which
sooner or later compelled them to renounce a faith that had

failed them. Although each of these "confessions" is fascinating, in none is the sense of betrayed hope more graphically stated than in Mr. Koestler's allusion to Jacob and Leah.

Painful as Mr. Koestler's misadventures must have been, his "Lost Weekend in Utopia" was by no means wholly lost. Out of those seven years (1931–38) of strange assignments, mysterious meetings, two imprisonments, journeys to Russia and Spain, and acquaintanceship with stalwart revolutionists who were fated to be executed after trials that were mockeries of justice, came *Darkness at Noon*. And few would dispute, unless as card-carrying Party members they were forced to do so, that this novel, which Sidney Kingsley has now dramatized,* is one of the finest to have emerged from our tumultuous times.

A decade has passed since *Darkness at Noon* was published. But the years, which bury books unmercifully, have not been able to rob Mr. Koestler's novel of its life. Although its initial impact was tremendous, its power continues undiminished. As a matter of fact, with each rereading *Darkness at Noon* seems the more remarkable. It stands the test of renewed scrutiny. Familiarity with it breeds only mounting admiration. The muscularity of its thinking, the skill of its planning, the vividness of its characterizations, the adroitness with which it shuttles from past to present, and the sense it creates of inhabiting a tortured mind (indeed, many minds, including the reader's) while it is laying bare the horrors of a governmental dream which has become a nightmare—all of these are merits that

* *Darkness at Noon*, a dramatization by Sidney Kingsley of the novel by Arthur Koestler. Staged by Mr. Kingsley. Settings and lighting by Frederick Fox. Costumes by Kenn Barr. Associate producer, May Krishner. Presented by the Playwrights' Company. With a cast including Claude Rains, Walter J. Palance, Alexander Scourby, Philip Coolidge, Richard Seff, Allan Rich, Kim Hunter, Herbert Ratner, Norman Roland, Will Kuluva, Geoffrey Barr, etc. At the Alvin Theatre, New York City. Opened January 13, 1951.

stand out more unmistakably on the fourth reading than on the first.

Equally notable is the manner in which Mr. Koestler has avoided the usual stencils and the expected physical brutalities a propagandist would have relied on. He was writing from disenchantment, no doubt from sorrow and anger too, about a topical event. He shared the outrage which rocked the world when the so-called Moscow Trials made a gauze transparency of that dividing curtain now spoken of as being iron. His, however, must have been a special fury when, as one of the enraptured, he was forced to realize that the cause upon which he had squandered his ardors was a Leah, not a Rachel. His book was dedicated to the memory of the men he had known personally who were victims of those trials. He had every reason for allowing bitterness to get the better of his skill and scorn to submerge his craftsmanship. But Mr. Koestler, being the exceptional writer he is, did more than keep himself and his materials under control. He was able to transform what in lesser hands could easily have provided the stuffs of indignant journalism into a work of art.

His story of how Rubashov, an old and famous Communist, is imprisoned and put to death for crimes of which he was innocent, is a masterly piece of work. No book of the many I have read on Soviet Russia or Communism has demonstrated so memorably how the Communist intellect, in or out of prison, is always imprisoned. None has shown in terms more terrifying how in Stalin's Russia the "means" have become the "ends." None has presented more graphically the cleavage which divides the older Party members from the younger generation they have spawned, a generation born (in Rubashov's phrase) without an umbilical cord.

The excellences of Mr. Koestler's novel are many. Among these count the sweep of its narrative, the firm sketching of its vignettes, the expert use it makes of small sensory details such as the smell of Gletkin's revolver belt, the tension of its cross-examinations, its depiction of the miseries and hungers of those who huddle in prison cells, and the brilliance with which it gets at the very essence of ideas. No feature of the book, however, is more admirable than Mr. Koestler's delineation of Rubashov. He is drawn without sentimentality, a figure every bit as ruthless as his opponents. His final tragedy is that though he has come to see the Party's faults he cannot forsake its precepts. He dies a perpetuator of the lie, fully aware of the crimes that are, yet willing to confess to crimes he himself has not committed.

Almost inevitably some of the literary qualities of *Darkness at Noon* have been mislaid in the process of bringing it to the stage. This was bound to be so, considering the very form and nature of the novel. Even so, and to a degree I would have thought impossible, Mr. Kingsley has succeeded in both his production and his dramatization in turning a fine book into an exciting and distinguished evening in the theatre.

Mr. Koestler may be a man of genius and Mr. Kingsley a man of ingenuity. In the world behind the footlights, however, Mr. Kingsley's ingenuity is not to be underestimated. He is a technician of outstanding abilities. His instinct for the stage is keen, his mastery of its means genuine. He happens to be a realist of the most painstaking sort. Everyone who saw *Men in White*, *Dead End*, or *Detective Story* must remember his inclination to hold the pier glass rather than the hand mirror up to nature. His fondness for the gadgets of realism remains undisguised even in *Darkness at Noon*. Occasionally it is responsible for details which are irrelevancies, such as the carefully furnished flashback scenes and the scrupulous painting of every stone on the transparencies that now serve as the walls of Rubashov's prison.

A little more imagination, a bolder use of suggestion, and less devotion to the Belasco trappings would no doubt have heightened Mr. Kingsley's production and made it theatrically more arresting. He has, however, been fortunate in having as his designer Frederick Fox, who is his equal in ingenuity. Mr. Fox has contrived a multiple setting which solves with startling ease the problem (and quite a housing problem it is) of containing not only Rubashov's cell and cells for some of his fellow prisoners but of allowing the drama to wander about from locale to locale as swiftly as Rubashov's memories or his present experiences. As a director Mr. Kingsley has also kept things moving. His script may lag in the second act and the sequences with the betrayed secretary may seem to take on an unintended importance. But Mr. Kingsley's direction is incisive and contributive throughout, and rises to haunting climaxes in those scenes when all the prisoners start beating upon their cell walls at once and their despairing protests find an eloquent release.

The major performance of the evening is, of course, Claude Rains's Rubashov, and it turns out to be one of the major performances of the season. Always a good actor, Mr. Rains has sometimes in the past been tempted to be too much of an actor. His Rubashov, however, never gets out of hand. It is beautifully controlled and modulated, underplayed rather than overplayed, and doubly effective for this very reason. The demands of the part are backbreaking. Quite aside from what it represents as a feat of memory, its other requirements for concentration are merciless. Yet Mr. Rains manages to meet all these tests triumphantly. The iron of Rubashov is in him, the knife-like quality of his mind, the habit of command, and the force that is his.

The human being is also there, alive though submerged, but guilty of thinking and feeling at moments in terms of the first person singular. This is a sin according to the Party. It is a bourgeois weakness which Mr. Koestler described as "the grammatical fiction." Nonetheless, the fact that Rubashov is a man no less than a Communist, even though an individual stifled and ultimately self-erasing because of loyalty to the Party, is a source of the strength both of Mr. Rains's playing and Mr. Koestler's and Mr. Kingsley's writing.

I notice that some of my confreres have complained because in his dramatization Mr. Kingsley has named the USSR as the setting of his play whereas Mr. Koestler specified no country in his novel. Surely this is an illogical objection. Mr. Koestler's dedication made clear beyond doubt the scene he had in mind. So, for that matter, did the story he had to tell on each of its haunting pages. It would seem a little late in the day for liberals, no matter how liberal, to pretend to themselves that *Darkness at Noon* is laid in Cuckoo-Borough-on-Clouds. It is, alas, anchored in reality and its truth is part of its power.

February 3, 1951

*THE TERRIBLE plight of the artist
in Soviet Russia, and the stirring speech
with which Meyerhold courageously
chose to end his career.*

≈≈≈≈≈≈≈≈≈≈≈≈≈≈≈≈≈≈≈≈≈≈≈≈≈≈≈≈≈≈≈≈≈

"People's Artist"

AT THE third cross-examination Gletkin had said, "Your testimony at the trial will be the last service you can do the Party." He was speaking to Rubashov, one of the revered makers of the Revolution, who was facing sentence of death on some trumped-up charges of counterrevolutionary activities. As everyone knows who has read Arthur Koestler's *Darkness at Noon* or seen Sidney Kingsley's dramatization of it, Rubashov did go to his death, having performed his final service to the Party by telling the expected lie.

"Citizen Judges," he had said at the travesty of justice which was his trial. "Citizen Judges, covered with shame, trampled in the dust, about to die, I will describe to you the sad progress of a traitor, that it may serve as a lesson and terrifying example to the millions of our country. . . ."

Such words of self-abasement have a familiar ring. They fit into a pattern the contemporary world has come to know all too well. They may still seem incredible to men whose minds are free. They may sicken those who live in countries accustomed to prizing the individual. Even so, every sudden shift in the Kremlin's policy, every purge that such a shift has brought about, and every public trial staged in Moscow have forced us in spite of the stubbornness of our disbelief to expect such a crumbling of will and distortion of truth.

If I come back to Rubashov and *Darkness at Noon,* it is because I have been reading with fascination and a heavy heart *Taming of the Arts.** This is a backstage account of what happened between 1930 and 1940 to music and the theatre under the Soviet dictatorship. Its author is Juri Jelagin, a Russian-born violinist, who was intimately acquainted with the artists of Moscow. Formerly he was attached to the Vakhtangov Theatre. He then became a member of the Moscow Conservatory. As a soloist, his concerts carried him on tours even to Siberia. During the war he was captured by the Germans and deported. Since then he has come to this country and is now with the Houston Symphony.

In Mr. Jelagin's pages can be found the words spoken publicly by another famous revolutionary figure when he, too, had fallen into disfavor. In this instance the speaker was not a fictional character. He was Vsevolod Meyerhold, one of the modern theatre's best known directors, the first important manager to proclaim himself a Communist in the days of the Revolution, and a leader of the Soviet stage so outstanding that he had long since been made a "People's Artist."

There are hundreds of incidents in *Taming of the Arts* dealing with the strange and unhappy experiences of such artists as Stanislavsky, Tairov, Kachalov, Maxim Gorky, Aleksey Tolstoy, Vakhtangov, and Shostakovich, which tempt me to touch upon them. There are stories which I find hard to resist retelling about Stalin, his sudden telephone calls, his likes and dislikes in music and the drama, and the ordeal of an actor

* *Taming of the Arts,* by Juri Jelagin. Translated from the Russian by Nicholas Wreden. New York: E. P. Dutton & Co., Inc. 333 pp. $3.50.

who understandably lost his voice when he had to impersonate Uncle Joe with Stalin in the audience. There is the cumulative picture, drawn unforgettably by Mr. Jelagin, of the dizzying privileges, the abrupt reprimands, merciless dismissals, and general uneasiness of Soviet artists that I should like to discuss at length. If I single out Meyerhold's story and concentrate upon it I have my personal reasons for doing so.

I met Meyerhold three or four times in Paris in the distant summer of 1928. He was then at the height of his power, an imperious-looking man to whom command came naturally. His face was thin and decisive. There was no mistaking his force or the fact that he was accustomed to acclaim. He was so highly regarded by his government that his theatre had been chosen to represent the USSR at the International Season Gémier was holding at the Odéon. How I met him I cannot remember, but I also met his actress-wife, Zinaida Raikh, a pretty brunette who, as I recall her, resembled a somewhat plump version of Pola Negri. With the aid of a French woman who acted as interpreter we managed to carry on the semblance of conversations.

I was then a recent graduate of the staff of the old *Theatre Arts Monthly* and was very anxious to go to Russia in order to study its stage. I had tried without success in London, Stockholm, Copenhagen, and Berlin to get permission to enter the Soviet Union in those days when we had no diplomatic relations. Had it not been for Meyerhold my request would have been turned down again in Paris. He, however, was kind enough to take my case in hand, and I soon realized how powerful his hand was.

He took me to the Soviet Embassy, put in a long distance call to Moscow, and within a few days I received my permit. It was as simple as that. Meyerhold's helpfulness did not stop there. He insisted, since he would be in Paris, that my friend and I should stay at his apartment in Moscow during the two weeks we were allowed to remain in Russia. On our arrival his secretary met us with a car at the airport, and everything during our visit was made the easier because of the magic of his name.

All this, as I say, was in 1928. At that time the Soviet theatre, in spite of its wearisome preoccupation with propagandist themes, was extraordinarily stimulating in its production techniques. Its vitality was tremendous. Its importance as a means of mass instruction was recognized by the authorities. Its artists enjoyed exceptional privileges. Its offerings were of many kinds and styles. The battle line had not yet been drawn between "bourgeois formalism" and "socialistic realism," whatever those mystifying terms may mean.

In that throbbing world of the Soviet stage no person was more dominant or more respected than Meyerhold. He was the high priest of the revolutionary theatre, the innovator of innovators, the radical of radicals, the champion of Constructivism, and the creator of such renowned experimental productions as his tradition-destroying *The Inspector-General* and *Roar China!* He had won the idolatry of the Party's leaders by asking actors not to look upon themselves as stars but as "instruments for social manifestoes," by relegating to the past the "soul junk" and "rickety ego" of bourgeois characters, and insisting that what mattered most behind the footlights was the glorification of the "unindividual."

Meyerhold's apartment, in which I stayed, may have been a squalid, bug-infested, and dreary dump. But the government was building a beautiful new apartment house for him and his company. It was also planning to reward him by constructing a brand new playhouse, startling in its unorthodoxies. Though the ground was broken for this new theatre in 1934, the building was never to be completed. For soon thereafter Meyerhold himself was to learn how treacherous is the quicksand of official Soviet approval.

Mr. Jelagin reminds us that the atmosphere in Moscow began to change in 1934 when Kirov, one of Stalin's closest friends, was murdered. Two years later the terror was felt by everyone. Arrests were wholesale. The first of the great public trials had taken place. The one-time head of the NKVD had been arrested and the merciless Nikolai Yezhov had replaced him. Theatre after theatre became suspect. Shostakovich, who later was to recant in words very similar to Rubashov's, was denounced. Meyerhold enjoyed no immunity. He too was castigated. In 1936 he had dared to present his wife in a production of *Camille* which was sensitive and restrained and innocent of all the expected stunts. About the same time for the Leningrad opera he staged Tchaikovsky's *Queen of Spades* in an equally restrained manner.

Instantly *Pravda* turned its guns upon him. His theatre was described as being "foreign." Meyerhold was denounced as "the father of formalism." He was charged with having exercised a pernicious influence on other directors. He was singled out as the spokesman for hostile, anti-national tendencies. He was condemned for his desecrations of the classics. Most terrible of all, it was pointed out that in 1920 he had dedicated one of his productions to Leon Trotsky. Mr. Jelagin tells us that a few days after the appearance of the *Pravda* denunciation the Party took action. Meyerhold's theatre was liquidated by government decree, and the Committee on Arts ordered all the playhouses in the Soviet Union to hold meetings at which actors and directors were to condemn Meyerhold and endorse the government's procedure.

Meyerhold himself was not arrested. Being out of favor, however, meant that he was out of work. The only person in Moscow brave enough to offer him a job was old Stanislavsky. Meanwhile the imprisonments and executions of artists multiplied. By 1938 it began to seem, according to Mr. Jelagin, as if the government were prepared to forgive Meyerhold. His name started to reappear in the press uncoupled with such adjectives as "formalistic" or "decadent." In June, 1939, he was even asked by the Committee on Arts to be one of the speakers at the First National Convention of Theatrical Directors soon to be held in Moscow. On the night of the meeting the auditorium was filled to overflowing. Everyone's expectation was that Meyerhold would follow the weasel's course, denounce his own work, praise his persecutors, and promise to reform. But Meyerhold could not bring himself to do what Shostakovich and many others have done. There was no Rubashov blood in him.

After two preliminary addresses the chairman announced, "The next speaker is Vsevolod Meyerhold." The auditorium rocked with applause. When Meyerhold appeared behind the desk, briefcase in hand, a tired, gray-haired man, the ovation continued from artists who had forgotten their differences with him and fully sympathized with his dilemma. Then he began to speak. Mr. Jelagin, who was there, says he started slowly, in a low, deliberate voice. Little by little a light came into his eyes. Before long his strengthening tones had in them the ring of steel.

Although the whole of Meyerhold's speech, as Mr. Jelagin

has reported it, merits quoting, excerpts from it are enough to show how memorable it was. It was fierce in its integrity and thrilling in its courage.

Meyerhold began in the expected manner by seeming to admit his mistakes. Yet even when he enumerated them, it was clear that his spirit had not been broken. He spoke as an artist rather than a puppet. His old fire was not extinguished, his independence still flamed. His contempt for the inferior directors who had tried to imitate his style was as great as his pride in the best of his own work. His defiance grew with each bold sentence his conscience compelled him to utter. When he had failed, he said, he had done so only because he had exercised his right and need as a master to experiment.

With audacity he mentioned his "creative individualism." Next he mocked the mumbo-jumbo of such Communist aesthetic terms as "socialistic realism" and "anti-formalism." Then, knowing that his were self-destroying words, he rose magnificently to his peroration.

"I, for one, find the work in our theatres at present pitiful and terrifying. I don't know whether it is anti-formalism, or realism, or naturalism, or some other 'ism,' but I do know that it is uninspired and bad.

"This pitiful and sterile something that aspires to the title of socialistic realism has nothing in common with art. Yet the theatre is art, and without art there can be no theatre. Go to the Moscow theatres and look at the colorless, boring productions which are all alike and which differ only in their degree of worthlessness. No longer can anyone identify the creative signature of the Mali Theatre, of the Vakhtangov Theatre, of the Kamerni Theatre, or of the Moscow Art Theatre. In the very places where only recently creative life was seething, where men of art searched, made mistakes, experimented, and found new ways to create productions some of which were bad and others magnificent, now there is nothing but a depressing, well-meaning, shockingly mediocre, and devastating lack of talent.

"Was this your aim? If so you have committed a horrible deed. You have washed the child down the drain with the dirty water. In your effort to eradicate formalism you have destroyed art!"

What happened next? Meyerhold was arrested the following day and has never been heard from since. A few weeks later his wife was found in her apartment brutally murdered, with seventeen knife wounds in her body. The apartment was sealed by the NKVD and all personal property confiscated. In the autumn of that same 1939 a volume appeared in which a stenographic report was given of all the speeches made at that First Convention of Theatrical Directors. But, says Mr. Jelagin, Meyerhold's speech was missing and his name was not included in the list of those who attended. *Pravda,* to be sure, on June 15, 1939, had referred briefly to his appearance before the convention. This was the last time Meyerhold's name was mentioned in the Soviet press.

February 10, 1951

*GOOD AND EVIL in conflict on the
high seas, and the mystifying manner in
which the public stayed away from a fine
play made from Herman Melville's allegory about a doomed young sailor.*

Hanged from the Yardarm

IT HAS been rumored over the centuries that actors are not
opposed to having audiences. Why should they be? They
are not alone in wanting them, nor are dramatists, designers,
managers, "angels," and theatre owners the only ones who
share this taste. Playgoers also like audiences. They are happiest in jammed auditoriums. No heat produced by coal, oil,
or wood is more warming than that generated by the approval
and expectancy which a crowded house signifies. The fact that
every seat is taken, that the boxes bulge, and that standees are
plentiful means each person present must count himself lucky
to be present at all.

A theatre a third or a fourth filled is quite a different matter.
It is a lonely place. Dispiriting, too. It has a ghostly look. Even
before the house lights are dimmed its rows of unoccupied seats
resemble tombstones for hopes which have died.

I mention the cheerlessness of a sparsely populated playhouse because late in its short run I had the chilling experience
of seeing *Billy Budd* * acted before a handful of people. The

* *Billy Budd*, a new play by Louis O. Coxe and Robert Chapman, based on
the novel by Herman Melville. Directed by Norris Houghton. Settings by

smallness of the audience would have been depressing under any circumstances. In the case of this dramatization of Herman Melville's novel it was the more discouraging because here was a play and a production which, on the basis of interest and merit, should have had them "hanging from the rafters." It had everything in its favor—except the public which for three lean weeks had stayed away from it in droves.

I used to subscribe wholeheartedly to Emerson's mousetrap theory. But the fact that so few people beat a path to the theatre where *Billy Budd* was playing forces me to question it. The failure of *Billy Budd* dislodges another favorite assumption of mine. For years I have believed that a really good play can in the vast majority of cases live down bad notices. Here, however, was a really good play which good notices had not been able to help. Several of the daily critics had greeted it with ecstatic reviews. What is more, they had followed these up with no less ecstatic reappraisals. Yet "the boys," so often accused of breaking plays, could not make this one.*

The few who took their advice were enthusiastic. They were fully aware of the exceptional quality of what they were seeing. I know they were the night I saw *Billy Budd*. In the intermissions they discussed these merits on the sidewalk and in the lobby. They huddled together as defenders will, lamenting

---

Paul Morrison. Costumes by Ruth Morley. Presented by Chandler Cowles and Anthony B. Farrell. With a cast including Dennis King, Torin Thatcher, Charles Nolte, Guy Spaull, Jeff Morrow, Walter Burke, Jack Manning, George Fells, Bernard Kates, etc. At the Biltmore Theatre, New York City. Opened February 10, 1951.

* Due to the courage of the management, the cooperation of the cast in taking temporary cuts, and the last-minute enthusiasm shown by the public, the run of *Billy Budd* was extended for seven more weeks. Since then, it has been produced widely and with success by college, school, and off-Broadway organizations.

some of the trash that "packs them in" for months on end while such a work, so unusual in its virtues and dimensions, could starve to death in so short a time. "Can't something be done to save it?" I heard several people ask. But even those of us who would have been delighted to do our share in the saving sensed to our sorrow that this was a production beyond salvation, notwithstanding that everyone connected with it could be proud of it and that we who saw it had good reason to be proud of the theatre for having presented it.

Just what it was that kept ticket-buyers away from *Billy Budd* is impossible to determine with any precision. Was it because they were frightened by reading such adjectives as "stern," "grim," "austere," "intellectual"? These same words employed to describe *Darkness at Noon* had not scared them. Was it because (oh, eternal defense of those Philistines whose courage is little and whose minds are smaller) they surrendered to the death-dealing nonsense which holds life is so tragic nowadays that the theatre is obliged to be entertaining and nothing more? Was it because the title *Billy Budd* meant nothing to those who had not read Melville's allegory of Good and Evil? Or was it because playgoers could not steel themselves, in spite of glowing notices, to face the story of how a young sailor is unjustly hanged? Who knows? Who can say?

This I do know and this I can say. Those who did not see *Billy Budd* did their bit to discourage the theatre from doing its best. They turned their backs on courage and distinction. They helped the cause of cheapness and mediocrity, of the third-rate and the silly, a cause which, Heaven knows, has its overnumerous champions and needs no new recruits. Worst of all, they denied themselves an engrossing adventure.

The saga of Billy Budd was, of course, Melville's last work.

It was written when he had regained his self-belief after many painful years during which he had grown accustomed to being underestimated and neglected as an author. Although it was completed in 1891, the year of his death, when Melville was seventy-two, it was not published until 1924 and then in an inaccurate transcription.

In its first form it was cast as a short story called *Baby Budd, Sailor,* which F. Barron Freeman discovered only a few years back in Melville's chaotic manuscript and included in his scholarly edition of the novel.* The expansion of the 12,000-word short story into *Billy Budd, Foretopman,* which runs to 36,000 words, required a little more than two years. The result, though fragmentary, is beyond forgetting. It is distinguished by the same vividness of phrase, characterization, and narrative, the same sense of being as at home with the soul as with the sea, the same gift for prose which sings a song commonly beyond the reach of prose, and the identical altitude of meditation which glorify *Moby Dick.*

In *Moby Dick* the White Whale dwells in depths undreamed of by whalers. He is a symbol of destiny. He represents not only "the Nature man warily hunts and subdues," said Lewis Mumford, but that part of Nature which "threatens man and calls forth all his heroic powers" only to defeat him "with a final lash of the tail."

In similar fashion the concern of *Billy Budd* is far larger than a mere outline of its outward action might suggest. Though its setting is an English man-of-war, its subject refuses to be shipbound. It is a fable of Good and Evil and of

* *Melville's Billy Budd,* edited by F. Barron Freeman. The complete text of the novel with variant readings and of the unpublished short story. Cambridge: Harvard University Press. 1948. 381 pp. $5.

the hatred which goodness itself can create. It is an inquiry into the cold, impersonal forces of authority as they ignore and obliterate the individual who finds himself at odds with them. It is an incident at sea turned, as it were, into a morality play which deals with the compromises exacted by organized society and the injustices carried out in its interest and name.

When Melville wrote it he had three definite naval events in mind. Two of these were the Spithead and Nore Mutinies in the British fleet which in 1797 had created consternation in an England at war. The third came nearer home. It was the notorious "Mackenzie Case" which had shocked America in 1842. This case took its name from the captain who, in order to put down a rumored uprising on the U.S. brig-of-war *Somers*, had hanged three innocent sailors while still at sea. Inasmuch as Melville's first cousin had served as a lieutenant under Mackenzie, his was a personal interest in this unhappy incident.

Melville put these events to his own uses. It was not for nothing that he named the merchant vessel on which Billy Budd had sailed before his impressment *The Rights of Man* or that he christened the man-of-war upon which Billy met his untimely death the year after the Mutiny at the Nore the H.M.S. *Indomitable*. On page after page Melville's narrative is filled with overtones.

Billy, the Handsome Sailor, is the spokesman of the blind, the trusting, and the naive Good. His beauty is the external expression of his inner virtue, even as his stammer is a reminder of his human imperfection. Claggart, the master-at-arms, who hates him instinctively, is the embodiment of Evil, a born villain not a made one, a madman cool and crafty in his means and cursed with a genius for cruelty. It is his natural depravity which leads him to plot against Billy and accuse him unjustly of planning a mutiny. In the same way it is Billy's outraged innocence which, by causing him to stammer, makes it impossible for him to answer these false charges except by striking, and unintentionally killing, Claggart in the presence of Captain Vere.

The Captain is a bookish, thoughtful fellow, sardonic but likable, whose thinking is buttressed by strong convictions of duty. Although he has a father's fondness for Billy and knows him to be innocent of mutinous thoughts, he persuades the officers who try him that Billy must hang. He must hang because in wartime he has struck a superior, and according to the Mutiny Act that was a capital crime. He must hang because the crew, accustomed to stern discipline and remembering the Mutiny at the Nore, would mistake a more clement sentence for weakness. And hanged Billy Budd is, still struggling to believe in the justice of his fate and able to utter, as his surprising last words, "God bless you, Captain Vere."

The excitements of *Billy Budd, Foretopman* are sprung so surely from the fascination of Melville's digressions, his philosophical or descriptive passages, the power of his storytelling, and the sheer melody of his prose that I, for one, thought his short novel would resist dramatization. But, though certain of its qualities are bound to have been lost, Louis O. Coxe and Robert Chapman succeeded in turning it into an enthralling play. With an admirable awareness of the theatre's needs they extended the materials, supplying helpful scenes, clarifying motivations, incorporating new characters, developing the original ones, and writing dialogue that, while it remained remarkably faithful to the spirit and intention of the novel, possessed its own dramatic merits. They did not cheapen or compromise. They did not try to combine the easy sadism of *Mutiny on the*

Bounty with the rough-and-tumble talk of *Mister Roberts*. Instead, they wrote, and wrote skilfully, as men who understood and respected Melville at the same time that they understood and respected the stage.

This same integrity, skill, and understanding both of Melville and the theatre distinguished the entire production. They were manifest in Norris Houghton's extraordinarily able and sensitive direction. They were present in Paul Morrison's excellent settings. They also characterized the acting of the minor no less than the major parts. Dennis King, whose diction is blessed with a faultless precision, was a perfect Captain Vere—authoritative, kindly though aloof, and human until he must show himself to be the prisoner of regulations. Torin Thatcher's Claggart had all the driving, controlled, intellectual evil of Melville's master-at-arms. And Charles Nolte to an incredible degree managed to establish the trusting goodness of Billy without making him sappy.

"My books will speak for themselves," said Melville in his later years, "and all the better if I avoid the rattling egotism by which so many won a certain vogue for a certain time." No one can question that as a play *Billy Budd* spoke for itself. The pity is that it never won that "certain vogue for a certain time" which would have allowed it to speak to the large audiences it deserved.

March 17, 1951

WHEN A religious experience, pro-
found and radiant, and an adventure in
theatregoing happen to be one and the
same thing.

≈≈≈≈≈≈≈≈≈≈≈≈≈≈≈≈≈≈≈≈≈≈≈≈≈≈≈≈≈≈

The Ever Green Pastures

"**G**ANGWAY! Gangway for de Lawd God Jehovah!"
The modern theatre has produced no entrance cue
better known or more affectionately remembered. These are
words which even when read make the heart stand still. Heard
again in the theatre, heard in the world as it now is, their
impact is, if anything, greater than when they were spoken
twenty-one years ago in that other simpler and comparatively
civilized world in which *The Green Pastures* * was first produced.

When Marc Connelly finished his script, he had written a
far, far larger play than perhaps he realized. He had been
reading Roark Bradford's *Ol' Man Adam an' His Chillun,*
that delectable series of Bible stories as retold in the language
of devout but untutored Louisiana Negroes. He decided to

* *The Green Pastures,* a fable by Marc Connelly, suggested by Roark Bradford's Southern sketches, *Ol' Man Adam an' His Chillun.* Directed by Mr.
Connelly. Production designed by Robert Edmond Jones. Choir under the
direction of Hall Johnson. Presented by The Wigreen Company in association with Harry Fromkes. With a cast including William Marshall, Ossie
Davis, John Marriott, William Dillard, William Veasey, Rodger Alford,
Alma L. Hubbard, Alonzo Bosan, Vinie Burrows, Avon Long, Milroy In-
gram, John Bouie, etc. At the Broadway Theatre, New York City. Opened
March 15, 1951.

· 193 ·

dramatize these Old Testament tales "about the time when the Lord walked the earth like a natural man."

To do this, Mr. Connelly invented the device of a Sunday-school class and in its preacher, Mr. Deshee, he found a narrator whose human habit it was to visualize the wonders of the Good Book in terms of the everyday experiences he and his people had had. Mr. Connelly went further. Although in some of his scenes he relied on Mr. Bradford's enchanting episodes and phrases, he contributed not only new material but a new dimension to Mr. Bradford's sketches. Without losing their humor, a humor born of faith at its most innocent, he added a religious feeling as touching, as heart-sprung and all-conquering as that glorifying the spirituals which are an essential part of the production.

The resulting play may have been set in a Louisiana parish, but it shone with qualities which persuaded a whole nation to enroll among its parishioners. Delightful though it was as a work of art, it was more than an adventure in theatregoing. It was a religious experience of a profound and radiant sort. It still is. The years have not diminished its appeal.

No sermon has ever made goodness more contagious. Or so dispensed with preaching and the pulpit manner in illustrating what lies at the core of faith. Without irreverence it smiles in God's presence, worshipful but unterrified, and filled with the kind of happiness that in itself is an expression of love. If its virtuous mortals such as Noah, Moses, Hezdrel, and the rest are as unabashed when facing their Creator as are Gabriel, the cherubs, and the angels at the heavenly fish fry, it is because all of them, heaven- or earth-born, are at ease with Him.

And why not? De Lawd in *The Green Pastures* may describe himself to Noah as "a god of wrath and vengeance" but surely wrath never took so gentle a form. Although from time to time he has to punish erring mankind, he seems more saddened than outraged by the need to do so. Sin is something he "jest can't stan'." Yet an eye for an eye or a tooth for a tooth is not among his demands. In spite of having thunderbolts at his disposal, he does not throw his weight about. Instead, he is the kindliest of administrators, tolerant and benign.

The tremendous burden he carries casts its shadow on his spirit even if it leaves his back unbent. He is well aware that "bein' de Lawd ain't no bed of roses," but he never loses his patience, his serenity, or his dignity. He looks and talks like a mortal. Plainly, however, he is more than that. When Noah, who has not recognized him, confesses, "I should have known you. I should have seen de glory," he is telling the truth, for the glory is there. It is there in homespun, uncanonical terms, and never more so than in the beautiful last scene in which the Crucifixion is hinted at and de Lawd realizes that God, too, must learn mercy through suffering.

Quite rightly *The Green Pastures* has long since been saluted and accepted as a folk play. This in itself raises its convention-destroying points. For folk art is supposed to be the product of simple people. It is thought of as being country-bred, hence blessed with that innocence which a dubious tradition is fond of believing rural. It is held to be the expression of peasants, mountaineers, or naive artisans safely uncontaminated by any contact with cities or sophistication.

Although the Algonquin's Round Table, where the wags wagged and the "Vicious Circle" met, created its own lore, its members were scarcely of that jerkin, buckskin, or calico variety from which folklore springs. Mr. Bradford, a resident of New Orleans, did not belong to this group of latter-day Mermaid

Taverners, but Mr. Connelly did. He is one of the wittiest of city slickers and easily distinguishable from Johnny Appleseed. The fleshpots are not foreign to him. Yet these two very knowing men did manage to "r'ar back" and pass that miracle of folk art which *The Green Pastures* is.

No murals in a Dalecarlian home personalizing a Bible story in native dress could be less self-conscious and more honest. Nor could any miracle play in old Coventry have had a more compelling and unstudied purity. When the Custard Maker offers de Lawd a ten-cent seegar, he is following precisely the same impulse which prompted the adoring shepherds in *The Pageant of the Shearmen and Tailors* to present the Christ-Child with mittens, a pipe, and a hat.

No one who saw Richard B. Harrison during the five years that he appeared as de Lawd can have forgotten him. His was one of the modern theatre's most memorable performances, if, indeed, acting so seemingly free of calculation and so manifestly dependent upon the shining virtue of a man's own character can be described as a performance. Mr. Harrison's Jehovah added considerably "mo' firmament" to the lives of countless thousands of playgoers. His Lawd was elderly without being patriarchal; the perfect shepherd of a flock often lost and floundering; as human as the most mortal of his worshipers and yet possessed of some heaven-born goodness and authority.

The new Lawd of William Marshall is younger, a fact which in a world as overcrowded with problems as the present one is not without its consolations. His youthfulness (more accurately, his agelessness) of face endows him with an unwearied quality and speaks as comfortingly for his strength as does his giant size. Mr. Marshall does more, however, than tower physically above his angels and his earthlings. His dignity is no mere matter of physique. Human and lovable as he is, he too radiates "de glory," and radiates it abundantly.

Robert Edmond Jones's settings remain wonderful examples of the eloquence of simplicity. They have about them the same feeling of the morning of the world that so distinguishes the writing, the singing of the spirituals, and the production as a whole. Mr. Connelly's direction is once again inspired in the way in which it creates a lovely glowing reverence without ever being sanctimonious and manages to employ humor as a tender expression of devotion. Ossie Davis is an enchanting Gabriel; Alonzo Bosan a perfect Noah, impish but trusting; and John Marriott a profoundly moving Moses.

Let's face it with proper gratitude. *The Green Pastures* is a masterpiece. I came to recognize this early during its initial run and only wish I had had the sense to do so on the night of its opening. But then, to my shame, I missed the boat, which was quite a boat to miss considering it was the Ark. Though back in 1930 I saluted *The Green Pastures* as being brave and meritorious, I felt that, in spite of its charms and delights, it somehow fell short of its ultimate goal.

Perhaps my trouble was that when I first saw the play I had just finished reading Mr. Bradford's sketches and hence resented that grudging credit line which even now perplexes me by saying "suggested by" rather than "adapted from" or "based upon" Roark Bradford's book, *Ol' Man Adam an' His Chillun*. Or perhaps, being younger and far more academic, I was theatre-blinded and therefore guilty of judging a work of the spirit in dry technical terms.

Whatever my reasons may have been, this much I know: I was wrong. Not so wrong as that Bishop of the African Methodist Episcopal Church who, closing his eyes to the fundamentals of faith and the inherent sweetness of his people, has recently charged *The Green Pastures* with being "irreligious" and perpetuating "outmoded stereotypes" of Negroes. Even so, I was wrong. I was wrong because on that history-making first night I failed to recognize all that *The Green Pastures* represents dramatically, humanly, and spiritually.

April 7, 1951

A CERTAIN pug-nosed old Silenus, ugly on the outside but "all glorious within," as Plato captured his greatness and Maxwell Anderson has misplaced it.

ᴂ·ᴂ

Socrates without Plato

THERE is every reason why Maxwell Anderson, a passionate believer in democracy, should have been drawn to Socrates as the central figure in his most recent historical play.* With half the world overrun by dictatorships and individual freedom threatened even in this country, the squat, the ugly, pug-nosed, bearded old philosopher, who though a Silenus on the outside was "all glorious within," has as much to say to us as he did to ancient Athens because of his fate no less than his teachings.

Socrates was the kind of disconcerting character who in any age or country would put a civilization to the test. In Ibsen's fashion he was a self-appointed state-satirist, in Shaw's a professional gadfly. Mr. Anderson in his preface to *Barefoot in Athens* compares him in his earlier days to a Will Rogers of the market place. He enjoyed the same freedom, spoke with

* *Barefoot in Athens*, a new play by Maxwell Anderson. Directed by Alan Anderson. Settings and lighting by Boris Aronson. Costumes by Bernard Rudofsky. Presented by The Playwrights' Company. With a cast including Barry Jones, Lotte Lenya, George Mathews, Helen Shields, Philip Coolidge, William Hansen, David J. Stewart, Daniel Reed, William Bush, Bruce Hall, Bart Burns, etc. At the Martin Beck Theatre, New York City. Opened October 31, 1951.

the same terrifying sanity, and had something of the same sharpness of wit. Yet beyond this, as the years proved, Socrates was an incredibly persuasive teacher, a trained philosopher of the highest magnitude, and a great man who rose greatly to the martyrdom he finally faced in his seventieth year because of his lifelong championing of freedom of inquiry.

Like all men who have no interest in money Socrates was thought dangerous, and like all men who have an utter devotion to truth his contemporaries found him intolerable. Although he had demonstrated his personal bravery in battle to the approval of patriots, his intellectual courage enraged solid citizens. If he had a genius for winning ardent disciples, he had the same talent for winning enemies. Socrates was as modest about himself as he was relentless in asking questions, exploding misconceptions, and atomizing ideas. "Only one thing I know and that is that I know nothing," was his claim. Had he stopped there he would never have been brought to trial and sentenced to drink the hemlock. But his daily sport (really his lifework) was to prove to men who thought they were wise that they had no wisdom at all. This infuriated those he exposed and ultimately cost him his life.

Socrates excelled at logic, in itself a hazardous excellence, and was the inventor, in Mr. Anderson's phrase, of that question-and-answer game usually known as the Socratic method. As a teacher he was blessed in having Plato and Xenophon among those he taught and cursed in having Critias, Charmides, and Alcibiades, traitors all of them, who sold out to Persia or Sparta and thus aided in bringing about the fall of Athens—and Socrates. To hold him responsible for the misdeeds of his students was, of course, nonsensical. He loved his city so much that at the end he chose to die rather than to live elsewhere.

A healthy, democratic Athens (as Athens understood democracy) found Socrates embarrassing but put up with him; a defeated Athens found him unendurable and put him to death. The charges brought against him were that he had denied the old gods, introduced new ones of his own, and corrupted the thinking of youth. Though untrue, these charges were accepted as truth by the majority of the jury, for the times were against Socrates. Due to her defeat in the Peloponnesian War and her occupation by Spartan troops, Athens, as Mr. Anderson has pointed out, had grown fearful of the very spirit that produced her great men. The victory of such a Hitlerian or Communist dictatorship as Sparta had shaken her confidence in both freedom and herself. She wanted a scapegoat and found one in Socrates. By a vote of 281 to 220 he was judged guilty.

As surely as we depend upon Matthew, Mark, Luke, and John for the details of Christ's life, we depend (if we do not include Aristophanes's burlesque in *The Clouds*) upon Xenophon and Plato for what Mr. Anderson describes as the three gospels about Socrates. Why three gospels when only two men wrote them? Because Mr. Anderson believes that Plato had a change of heart and mind during his life that really made him two men. When he first employed his old teacher Socrates as his literary mouthpiece, or what Calvin Coolidge would have described as his Official Spokesman, Plato still believed in Socrates's teachings and Pericles's practice. But later on, as Xenophon proves to Mr. Anderson's satisfaction, Plato became "Socrates's Judas and turned against him and Athens," putting into his mouth fascist beliefs which, though they may have become Plato's, were never Socrates's.

There is little wonder that the Socrates we cherish is Plato's. Notwithstanding his distrust of artists and his willingness to have them curbed, Plato was himself one of the world's greatest literary artists. He had genius where Xenophon had good intentions. His Socratic dialogues are masterful pieces whereas the *Memorabilia* of Xenophon is a drearily pedestrian work, as everyone must admit who has read it. This is why the world has always turned to the author of the *Apology*, the *Crito*, and the *Phaedo* for the Socrates it venerates.

It is with this Plato that the author of *Barefoot in Athens* is forced to compete. Mr. Anderson is a fine man with the highest ideals. Again and again over his long career he has served the theatre admirably. He is a brave man, too. Sometimes, however, in choosing subjects for his historical plays his courage has misled him. It has tempted him to pit himself against the giants of literature. When he wrote about Henry VIII, for example, his play was bound to be compared to Shakespeare's on the same subject, even as when he wrote about a certain peasant maid his *Joan of Lorraine* had to contend with Shaw's *Saint Joan.* In the same way, the certainty that he would be inviting comparison with some of the finest and most moving passages in Plato has not kept Mr. Anderson from having Socrates his hero in *Barefoot in Athens* or from including a trial scene and a death scene doomed to be measured against the *Apology* and the *Phaedo.*

The boy, no matter how strong, who faces Goliath with a slingshot must be sure he is David before he goes into battle. No discourtesy is meant to Mr. Anderson in pointing out that he is no more the equal of Plato than he is of Shakespeare or Shaw. His *Barefoot in Athens* has its virtues. It can claim the interest of being built around a fascinating character. Its trial scene possesses the tension of important ideas. It contains some of the most straightforward dialogue Mr. Anderson has written in several years. Even when he falls back on Plato to paraphrase him, as he often does, he may not match the Greek's simple eloquence, but he does not obscure the strength of these borrowed speeches with fancy phrases.

Moreover, he reclaims Xantippe from those who have dismissed her merely as a shrew and creates a loving, hard-used woman who is excellently played by Lotte Lenya. The imaginary Spartan king, well acted by George Mathews, is likewise a well-conceived character, in spite of his strange desire to be addressed as "Stupid" and the incredible appearances he is forced to make in both the trial and death scenes after the Spartans have been expelled from Athens. Mr. Anderson also deserves credit for letting the parallels between the Athens of Socrates's last days and the contemporary world speak for themselves without being underscored.

Even so, *Barefoot in Athens* is a curiously drab and disappointing work. It is slow in getting started and awkward in some of its means. It lacks the needed fire. Although it is evocatively set by Boris Aronson, its direction is as unignited as its writing. Barry Jones is visually a fine Socrates. The humor and humanity of the great truth-seeker are his. All that his performance requires to become what it could be is the assistance of a text that is what it should be.

It is easy enough to describe a man as being great, but quite a different thing to demonstrate his greatness. It is this demonstrated greatness that is missing in Mr. Anderson's Socrates. He is shown as a word-juggler, a dangerous fellow to argue with. It is clear that he is a kind man, capable of quiet bravery, devoted to his city, and understandably trying to his family.

Yet somehow he remains more trivial than sizable. The agility of his mind is suggested but not its dimensions. Although the gadfly is present, the philosopher is absent.

As a case in point take the final prison scene. Plato's version of that last day in Socrates's life is one of the most memorable of all death scenes, second only to the accounts of the Crucifixion in its majesty and eloquence. As Mr. Anderson writes it, the heart-tearing serenity and the glory of the old man's dying disappear. It does not matter that Mr. Anderson chooses to have Socrates die at dawn instead of at sunset after a day of noble discussion, as he did in Plato's account. Nor does it matter, I suppose, that Mr. Anderson drops his curtain before the hemlock has begun to work and hence feels free to supply a final speech of his own writing. What does matter is that where Plato shows us a Socrates who, as a philosopher, spent his last hours seeking to prove the immortality of the soul, Mr. Anderson's Socrates dies not as a philosopher but as a loving father, a loyal Athenian, an ardent democrat, and a sentimental husband.

Plato's Socrates took a brief farewell of Xantippe and his children. Mr. Anderson's spends most of his remaining time with Xantippe. He dies with his arms around her, repeating a prayer to Pan that he used to say for her years ago. The prayer, which is a good enough one, runs: "Beloved Pan, and all you other gods who haunt this city, give me beauty in the inward soul, for outward beauty I'm not likely to have. May I reckon the wise to be the wealthy and those who need least to be most like the gods. Make me content with what I have but not self-satisfied. Let me give more than I get, love more than I hate, and think more of living than of having lived."

That is not the way Plato's Socrates dies. Neither, I suspect, is it the way Socrates would have chosen to die. Compare Plato's writing of the scene. In it Socrates dies in the company of his followers. Phaedo is speaking:

"He put the cup to his lips and drank the poison quite calmly and cheerfully. Till then most of us had been able to control our grief fairly well; but when we saw him drinking, and then the poison finished, we could do so no longer; my tears came fast in spite of myself, and I covered my face and wept for myself: it was not for him, but at my own misfortune in losing such a friend. Even before that Crito had been unable to restrain his tears, and had gone away; and Apollodorus, who had never once ceased weeping the whole time, burst into a loud cry, and made us one and all break down by his sobbing and grief, except only Socrates himself. 'What are you doing, my friends?' he exclaimed. 'I sent away the women chiefly in order that they might not offend in this way; for I have heard that a man should die in silence. So calm yourselves and bear up.'

"When we heard that we were ashamed and we ceased from weeping. But he walked about, until he said that his legs were getting heavy, and then he lay down on his back, as he was told. And the man who gave the poison began to examine his feet and legs, from time to time: then he pressed his foot hard, and asked if there was any feeling in it; and Socrates said, No: and then his legs, and so higher and higher, and showed us that he was cold and stiff. And Socrates felt himself, and said that when it came to his heart he should be gone. He was already growing cold about the groin, when he uncovered his face, which had been covered, and spoke for the last time. 'Crito,' he said, 'I owe a cock to Asclepius; do not forget to pay it.' 'It shall be done,' replied Crito. 'Is there anything else that you wish?' He made no answer to this question; but after a short interval there was a movement, and the man uncovered him, and his eyes were fixed. Then Crito closed his mouth and his eyes.

"Such was the end, Echecrates, of our friend, a man, I think, who was the wisest and justest, and the best man that I have ever known."

That is the Socrates of the *Phaedo*. It is not the Socrates of *Barefoot in Athens*.

November 24, 1951

THE SPECTACULAR rise of Julie Harris, and a tale about young people so self-absorbed that in the Berlin of 1930 they failed to see signs of the world's approaching tragedy.

Deserved Acclaim

IF THERE were no other reason for seeing *I Am a Camera* * (and there are many), Julie Harris would supply one. It is no pallid reason either. It is not the kind of weak summons which mere talent or competence issues. It is far more commanding than that. More exciting, too. Because, there's no sense beating around the bush, Miss Harris is a young actress blessed unmistakably with genius.

Everyone who saw her as the dream-struck adolescent in *The Member of the Wedding* was forced to realize she was no ordinary player. Her gawky little egotist, with her cropped hair, her unbecoming clothes, her disconcerting lack of manners, was an unforgettable performance. If it jangled the nerves, it also tore the heart. It was a full-length portrait of youthful loneliness. Its honesty, like its skill, was inescapable.

---

* *I Am a Camera*, by John van Druten, adapted from Christopher Isherwood's *The Berlin Stories*. Directed by Mr. van Druten. Setting by Boris Aronson. Costumes by Ellen Goldsborough. Presented by Gertrude Macy in association with Walter Starcke. With Julie Harris, William Prince, Martin Brooks, Catherine Willard, Olga Fabian, Edward Andrews, and Marian Winters. At the Empire Theatre, New York City. Opened November 28, 1951.

Dramatis Personae

Fine as Miss Harris's Frankie was, there was no telling where it would lead. Young actors often find themselves in parts which are just right for them and at which they therefore excel. During the year of their good fortune they are roundly and correctly praised. Then other seasons follow and things begin to go wrong. They never find the right part again or prove right in the parts which come their way. Gradually they sink out of sight, dashing the hopes which they had raised. They are like one-book authors. They do not have in themselves those rich reserves and that staying power which are indispensable to the making of a genuine career.

Miss Harris is different. Her Sally Bowles in *I Am a Camera* has nothing in common with her Frankie—except excellence. In looks, manner, voice, gestures, and stance she is another person; a character no less complete, but completely changed. Where her Frankie was naive, her Sally is experienced. Although a tart by temperament and practice, she is fundamentally a lady. There is a gentility about her which her uninhibited habits and vocabulary cannot disguise. Her availability has somehow left her innocence uncorrupted.

Being a human being, she seethes with contradictions. She is generous yet selfish, heartless but kind, and one of those mortal chameleons whose nature is always taking on the color of a new scene, a new mood, or a changed attitude. She is a night club singer who dreams of being a great actress and who never stops acting. She lives on a diet of self-sustaining lies. At one moment she is in a champagne mood, flamboyant, brandishing a cigarette, and striking sophisticated glamour-girl poses. At the next she is an eager young girl, seemingly simple and honest in spite of being as capricious as ever.

All these variations present challenges to Miss Harris which she meets so triumphantly that they do not seem challenges at all. She is able to make the difficult appear easy and to act as a virtuoso without calling attention to her acting. Moreover, in the process of creating Sally Bowles, Miss Harris creates something else. It is a strong faith in her ability; a conviction that she could play almost any part; an awareness, which grows from scene to scene, of being in the presence of a true and important actress.

The play, made memorable by Miss Harris's performance, has been wheedled by John van Druten from Christopher Isherwood's *The Berlin Stories*. Certainly, to those who have not seen it, no title could seem more awkward than *I Am a Camera*. Yet, clumsy as it is, it has its point and explains itself early in the evening.

Mr. van Druten's is a script which seeks to avoid that tidying up, hence distortion, of life which is the expected and accepted feature of a carefully plotted drama. He is writing with deliberate casualness about a group of young people who go their way in the Berlin of 1930 without realizing, at first, the sinister forces already at work in a city where their search is pleasure.

These young people include a Jewish girl; a gigolo who is Jewish but does not admit it; an eccentric American millionaire who fails to fulfill his promises of extravagant gifts and world tours; and Sally Bowles's English compatriot and friend who is known, somewhat embarrassingly, as Christopher Isherwood. In addition to being a character, this friend is the play's narrator. He explains the aim and method of Mr. van Druten's writing when he describes himself as a passive observer who records what he sees and hears with no more editorial selection than a camera with its shutter open.

Although a process supposedly as non-selective as this is

bound to result in some pictures which are out of focus, the experiment more than justifies itself. Whatever its faults may be, the play is never dull. Its best scenes are fresh and sensitive and have a fine honesty. They have that unposed, spontaneous quality which can endow a snapshot with a vitality unknown to most studio portraits.

Few characters I can remember have been drawn as candidly as Sally Bowles. Part of her validity is that she is left unresolved and that her inconsistency is shown as her chief consistency. For this very reason she may confuse those who are accustomed to having people denied their complexity as soon as they are turned into "characters." Yet it seems to me a great relief to encounter a character who is not all good or bad, generous or selfish, vulgar or refined, and who, instead of being as neatly wrapped as a Christmas package, is left as disordered as she would be in life.

There are other aspects of the writing of *I Am a Camera* which I admire and for which I am grateful. One is the truth with which it makes clear how most of us stumble from day to day with a vision as limited as a kodak's, seeing only what is in front of us, caring only for what concerns us, and often remaining strangely unchanged even by world affairs which can toss our lives about like leaves in a gale.

Mr. van Druten is no less effective in his quiet suggestions of Nazi barbarism already showing itself in the Berlin of 1930. No Brownshirts appear, and none of the physical violence to be found in most plays dealing with Nazism occurs on stage. A landlady, kindly by temperament but already parroting the anti-Semitic propaganda she has heard from soapbox orators; mention of the public funeral of a dead leader; and a bruise on the cheek of the Jewish girl, caused by a rock thrown by some of Hitler's hoodlums—these are the indirect means by which Mr. van Druten creates the sense of the condemned Berlin in which his characters move. They are enormously touching, particularly in the case of the Jewish girl who is played with heartbreaking simplicity by Marian Winters. The monumental tragedy of her people and stupid inhumanity of the Nazis are eloquently communicated by a bruise small enough to be covered by a Bandaid.

Mr. van Druten's direction is masterly in its eye for details and its sense of small values and their larger overtones. It is wonderfully knowing, human, and civilized. Boris Aronson's Berlin boarding-house is, too, a perfect background for the lighthearted Bohemia it menaces with a heavy Deutsch atmosphere.

The cast, with one exception, is no less contributive. William Prince succeeds admirably in turning into positive virtues the negative "big brother" qualities of Sally Bowles's loyal friend and counselor. Edward Andrews is as funny as only an American can be when seen through European eyes, and Olga Fabian is a warmhearted and mothering landlady. My single quarrel with the production comes with the casting of Catherine Willard as Sally Bowles's mother. Miss Willard gives a straight stock company performance. She is blowzy and hardboiled where she needs to be tweedy and "county." She, therefore, adds confusion to the evening by failing to explain the difference between Sally's present pursuits and her conventional background.

I trust I have indicated the shortcomings and the virtues of *I Am a Camera.* Both are present. Of the two, however, the virtues seem to me to be far the more important. Among these virtues count not only the fascination of the better scenes and the general excellence of the performance, but also the sheer magic of Miss Harris's acting. So far as she is concerned, play-goers are bound to feel something of that excitement which astronomers must know when a new star shines before their eyes.

December 22, 1951

THE WAY promotions are won, or the trials an ambitious young couple must put up with in order to get ahead as good Americans should.

꒰ꍈ꒱ꍈ꒱ꍈ꒱ꍈ꒱ꍈ꒱ꍈ꒱ꍈ꒱ꍈ꒱ꍈ꒱ꍈ꒱ꍈ꒱ꍈ꒱ꍈ꒱ꍈ꒱ꍈ꒱ꍈ꒱

Success Story

"**I** AM the master of my fate, I am the captain of my soul." We all know Henley's lines. Their assurance thunders in our ears. They restore importance, dignity, and independence to the individual. They say what we would like and need to believe. They tell us we are doomed only if we doom ourselves. Since they put each man's destiny under his own control, naturally we find comfort in their confidence. But, as *Point of No Return* * makes clear, though we may be captains of our souls we are not necessarily masters of our fates. At least we are not on those lower echelons of daily living which yield us bread and bring promotions.

No one who has to have his boss for dinner is completely free. No one whose hopes for a raise in salary and position depend upon the whims of those above him is a true master of his fate. The bent will like the bent back is a form of slavery. Few

---

* *Point of No Return*, a new play by Paul Osborn, based on John P. Marquand's novel. Directed by H. C. Potter. Settings by Jo Mielziner. Costumes designed by Main Bocher, assisted by Frank Spencer. Presented by Leland Hayward. With a cast including Henry Fonda, John Cromwell, Leora Dana, Frank Conroy, Colin Keith-Johnston, Robert Ross, Bartlett Robinson, Patricia Smith, Phil Arthur, etc. At the Alvin Theatre, New York City. Opened December 13, 1951.

worshipers of "the bitch-goddess, Success," will admit this openly. To do so would be unwise, and doing so would not get anyone anywhere. The realists recognize life is like that and accept it on its own terms. They grin and bear the fact that apple-polishing is as much in order in the office as it was in the schoolroom. They know that, to conquer, a little stooping has to be done and a lot of "yes, sirs" have to be said regardless of the "no, sirs" that may be thought.

Yet even the young hopefuls and their wives, who pretend not to mind the kowtowing which oils the way to fatter salaries, doubtless have their private moments of revolt. The boredom and the bowing, to which they have no other choice than to submit if they want one day to bore and to be bowed to themselves, must have taught them the poignant truth so agreeably stated in Paul Osborn's dramatization of John Marquand's novel. This is that the man who climbs assumes the same position as the man who crawls.

The climbing or the crawling described with such warmth and insight in *Point of No Return* is twofold. For the play, like the book, is concerned with scaling the ladder not only in New York but also in a small caste-bound New England town. This is why few husbands and few wives, young or old, can sit before the play without finding a part of themselves in it; without having a memory stirred, an experience relived, or an emotion completely shared. It is a sort of "Everyman" about white-collardom, the story of all properly ambitious young men who, in the stock phrase, seek to forge ahead or dream of becoming an officer in their company.

The full richness of Mr. Marquand's novel is lacking. Considering the book's length and variety of incident, this was bound to be. What I was unprepared for, however, is how much of the tone, narrative, atmosphere, and feeling of the original Mr. Osborn has managed to squeeze into his dramatization.

The last book by Mr. Marquand to reach the stage was *The Late George Apley* as adapted by George S. Kaufman. The result was a very entertaining evening which, though good theatre, was indifferent Marquand. Certain clear-cut differences in temperament and endowment seemed to separate Mr. Marquand and Mr. Kaufman. Gifted as they both are as writers, the one as a satirist, the other as a wisecracker, Mr. Marquand was so much the spokesman of Boston and Mr. Kaufman of Broadway that, as I tried to point out, only the New York, New Haven and Hartford Railroad connected the two men.

Mr. Osborn comes much closer to sharing Mr. Marquand's point of view and touch. When we recall such of his own comedies as *The Vinegar Tree, Oliver Oliver,* and *Morning's at Seven,* and such of his previous dramatizations as *On Borrowed Time* and *A Bell for Adano,* this is not surprising. In addition to being a proven craftsman, Mr. Osborn is a highly sensitive and subtle observer. Where Mr. Kaufman is a brilliant gagster and Times Square sophisticate, Mr. Osborn is a dramatist capable of tenderness no less than wit. In Mr. Marquand's fashion he is unfrightened by emotion. He appreciates good writing for good writing's sake and is able to translate it into theatrical terms so that its literary values are suggested.

The play he has derived from Mr. Marquand's book is certainly no masterpiece. It has its moments in the second act during its flashbacks to a New England town which must mean more to those who have read the novel than to those who have not. Its final scene, too, when the young couple entertain the president of the bank and his wife instead of going to their house for dinner, is not all it should be. It is awkward in its reliance on telephone calls and unconvincing in its attempt to prove that its central character has preserved his independence by refusing to follow the bank president's advice and join a certain country club.

Even so, *Point of No Return* is a more than competent job. In terms of the social strata classified in it by one of its own characters, an anthropologist, it may be "middle upper-class" rather than "upper upper-class," as Walter Kerr, the excellent new critic of the *Herald Tribune,* has pointed out. But "middle upper-class," so far as new plays go this season, is a very high high, and in any year *Point of No Return* would be a contribution welcome because of its humor and humanity.

It is distinguished throughout by the kind of professionalism which restores one's faith in the theatre. This professionalism is as apparent in the writing as it is in the settings, the direction, and the playing. *Point of No Return* includes five first-rate performances. Most prominent among these is, of course, Henry Fonda's ambitious young banker. Once again, as in *Mister Roberts,* Mr. Fonda manages to be charming and effective without seeming to act at all. Leora Dana is also wonderfully simple and believable as his realistic young wife. John Cromwell, all too long in Hollywood, is responsible as Mr. Fonda's father for the kind of characterization as shrewdly and quietly established as the one he gave years ago in *Lucky Sam McCarver.* Few character parts of recent seasons have been projected with greater vividness or skill than Robert Ross shows as the anthropologist. And Frank Conroy as the bank president is, as always, an adroit and authoritative player.

One important point the play misses, rewarding as it is and popular as it is certain to prove. This is the ironic swiftness with which, in Mr. Marquand's concluding pages, the young husband and wife, who have hoped for promotion, become accustomed to their new position once they have learned he is to be a vice president of the bank. Promotion, Mr. Marquand reminds us, is no guarantee of freedom. New responsibilities invite a new form of captivity. Even the vice presidents of banks are not masters of their fates.

January 5, 1952

Bang the Brasses

RICHARD RODGERS and Oscar Hammerstein 2nd continue to be unintimidated by their past successes, and prove that the most courageous of experimentalists can be those who desire and achieve hits.

Another Enchanted Evening

THEY HAVE done it again. Since "they" happen to be Richard Rodgers and Oscar Hammerstein, this is exciting news. What makes it the more exciting is that once again they have struck out in a new direction. Instead of trying in *The King and I* * to write another *South Pacific* or another *Carousel* or *Oklahoma!* they have written a musical as different from them as each of these was from the other.

This, of course, is as it should be but as it seldom is. Most toilers in the theatre are victimized by their past successes. If lucky enough to have found a formula that works, they use it over and over. The simple, perhaps the very human, truth is that fear of failure can make cowards of those who have

* *The King and I*, a new musical play with music by Richard Rodgers, book and lyrics by Oscar Hammerstein 2nd. Based on Margaret Landon's novel, *Anna and the King of Siam*. Directed by John van Druten. Settings by Jo Mielziner. Costumes by Irene Sharaff. Choreography by Jerome Robbins. Orchestrations by Robert Russell Bennett. Presented by Rodgers and Hammerstein. With a cast including Gertrude Lawrence, Yul Brynner, Dorothy Sarnoff, Doretta Morrow, John Juliano, Robin Craven, Larry Douglas, Johnny Stewart, Sandy Kennedy, etc. At the St. James Theatre, New York City. Opened March 29, 1951.

tasted success. Mr. Rodgers and Mr. Hammerstein, however, are exceptions. Although they have had—and deserved—successes which can only be described as triumphs, they have never been intimidated by them.

This raises an often ignored point about their extraordinary career as collaborators. The stage's experimentalists are commonly thought of as bright-eyed idealists who are happy to work for little in short-lived productions in small theatres safely removed from Broadway. The less they think of the box office the more they are supposed to think of their art. Meritorious failures are among their expectations and add prestige, if not luster, to their names.

In this respect, as in many another, Mr. Rodgers and Mr. Hammerstein are different. There is nothing long-haired or lily-clasping about them. Without talking about art they create it. They are professional Broadway show people who not only know their business but know it is a business. Their interest in their weekly grosses is realistic and hardboiled. A coterie is not their idea of an audience.

They frankly want to write hits, and hits are what they generally do write. Yet, in spite of being practical men blessed with the Midas touch, they are genuine experimentalists. Although their natural hope may be that others will like what they do, perhaps the real secret of their success is that they do what they themselves like in such a way that most often a huge public finds it impossible not to like it too. Regardless of the enormous investment each of their musicals represents, they are forever trying new things. Their courage is equaled only by their sagacity, taste, and skill.

All these qualities which distinguish Mr. Rodgers and Mr. Hammerstein lend distinction to *The King and I* and combine to make it the enchanting adventure in theatregoing that it is. Before touching upon the evening's charms, however, let me point out some of the proofs it supplies of its authors' adventurousness. First among these count the very fact that they decided to make a musical play from *Anna and the King of Siam*. For the problems were sizable which they had to solve, and have managed to solve brilliantly, in bringing to the stage that long and leisurely book by Margaret Landon in which she told of the liberalizing changes effected in the early 1860's when an English widow came to serve as governess to the innumerable children of a semi-barbaric Siamese despot.

Quite aside from such all-important matters as the selection of materials fitted to the needs of a swift-moving and simplified dramatization or the extent to which the music and atmosphere should be authentically Oriental, there were other difficulties to be met. Most musicals depend for their appeal upon love stories which end happily and in which the lovers, however thwarted, are admittedly in love. But Anna and the King are in love without knowing it or showing it except in an ebullient polka, though even that, in these post-Kinsey days, must be considered a minor manifestation of what Percy Hammond described as "the obstinate urge." Worse still, the King dies. Moreover, the historical Anna, though forceful, was more noteworthy for her earnestness than her glamour. The gray lady touch was on her spiritually. She was a "good woman," with all the forbidding and chilling qualities this implies. She had the right kind of bedside manner for a hospital and the wrong sort for a musical.

Mr. Rodgers and Mr. Hammerstein, however, are as ingenious as they are intrepid. Realizing they had a strong story to tell, they wisely disregarded the conventions of musical comedy and relied on the story's interest and their own abilities to make it satisfying and effective. Neither their boldness nor their acumen stopped there.

For their Anna they chose Gertrude Lawrence, a glittering and buoyant performer, who seemed to some of us in advance a precarious, if not a wrong, choice because of her very luster, vitality, and sophistication. Then they entrusted the pivotal task of staging *The King and I* to John van Druten, who, though noted for the skill with which he has directed plays, had had no previous experience with a musical. Each of these decisions was hazardous. Each involved a definite risk. Yet all of them, as is now apparent, were wonderfully right.

Good taste, the kind of perfect taste which characterizes the staging, the dancing, the performances, the settings, the costumes, and the writing of both the music and the book of *The King and I,* is one of the most uncommon attributes. One of the most delightful, too. It is a matter of control, of knowing when to stop, of refusing to allow tenderness to sink into sentimentality, and of realizing that beauty cannot be purchased by mere opulence.

It is the product of informed sensibilities and expresses itself in a thousand ways—in the colors and lines of a costume or a setting, in the phrasing of a speech, in the grouping of a scene, in the unfolding of a narrative, or in the happy blending of all these elements. It reveals itself as much by what is left out as by what is put in. It is no pallid or negative virtue. Certainly it is not as displayed by Mr. Rodgers, Mr. Hammerstein, and their co-workers. Instead, it is a positive and vital contributor to pleasure. Not in years has it been more blessedly present in any musical than in *The King and I.*

Although Mr. Rodgers may have produced lovelier tunes

in the past and Mr. Hammerstein may have written catchier lyrics, the two of them have never worked together more skilfully as master showmen or offered a production warmer in its feelings or more beguiling in its beauties. I, for one, wish that at least seven of the King's and the Prince's countless repetitions of "etcetera and etcetera" for comic purposes could be removed. I must admit, too, that I found the soliloquy a little long in which Miss Lawrence rehearses all the things she would like to say to the King. But there my quibbling comes to an abrupt end.

The reasons for my admiration are many and various. Among them permit me, in that hideous and un-Homeric "catalogue of the ships" which every reduction of a musical to a review represents, to enumerate the following. I thoroughly enjoyed such songs as "I Whistle a Happy Tune," "Hello, Young Lovers!" "Getting to Know You," and "Shall We Dance?" I delighted, as who could fail to, in the look, feel, and texture of the production; in the colorful excellence and yet the restraint of Jo Mielziner's Bangkok settings; and in the seductive loveliness and imagination of Irene Sharaff's costumes. Mr. van Druten's direction, so sure and quietly inventive in its touch, also commands respect. And so do the performances given by John Juliano as the Prime Minister; Larry Douglas and Doretta Morrow as the ill-fated secondary lovers; Dorothy Sarnoff as one of the King's wives; Johnny Stewart as the boy Prince; and Sandy Kennedy as Miss Lawrence's young son.

Let me quickly add that there are moments in *The King and I* which I shall always treasure. These include the irresistible innocence and delicacy of the scene in which the King's children are presented to Anna; the charm of the geography lesson; the joyous grace of Miss Lawrence's polka number; and the dignity with which the King's death is written and staged. Above all, I shall cherish the memory of Jerome Robbins's ballet, "The Small House of Uncle Thomas," in which Harriet Beecher Stowe's classic about slavery is pantomimed in the stylized terms of Siamese dancing. Surely this is creation, pure and inspired and utterly captivating.

I doubt if a more ideal King could have been found than Yul Brynner. He is the complete Oriental autocrat; a half-civilized monarch, gruff, rough, and accustomed to immediate and unquestioning obedience. He radiates a sense of power. Yet underneath the masklike exterior of the tyrant Mr. Brynner manages to suggest the human quality and the appeal of the submerged man.

As for Miss Lawrence, those of us who thought she would be wrong or wasted as Anna were, as I have indicated, wrong ourselves. The best analysis of Miss Lawrence's sparkling and kaleidoscopic gifts I have read is in Noel Coward's *Present Indicative*. "On the stage," wrote he, "she is potentially capable of anything and everything. She can be gay, sad, witty, tragic, funny, and touching. She can play a scene one night with perfect subtlety and restraint, and the next with such obviousness and overemphasis that your senses reel. She has, in abundance, every theatrical essential but one: critical faculty. . . . But for this tantalizing lack of discrimination she could, I believe, be the greatest actress alive in the theatre today."

This was written in 1937 by one who had the right to say, "I know her well, better, I believe, than most people." If my hope is that Mr. Coward will see Miss Lawrence in *The King and I*, my suspicion is that he will be amazed by her performance and delighted by it. Beyond question on the first night it was beautifully disciplined and controlled. The exuberant Miss Lawrence, the soignée or rowdy enchantress of the old days, the effervescent Gertie, the veritable Catherine wheel of comedy and song—all of these have, for the moment, gone underground to be replaced by a new Miss Lawrence.

Her incredible grace remains with her as she moves about in her great hoopskirts. So do her glamour, her beauty, and her charm. But this time she is never misled by them into forgetting the character she is creating. If as a person she is more colorful by far than the somewhat somber governess of Miss Landon's book, this is as it should and must be. Even so, her Anna has the dignity that comes from a quiet inner strength. She shines with goodness and yet is not mawkish. The truth is that her gentle and restrained Anna is one of the finest and least expected performances of Miss Lawrence's dazzling career.

April 14, 1951

*WHERE MEN are guys and girls are
dolls, or a delightful "Fable of Broadway" in which Damon Runyon comes
into his own behind the footlights.*

᪥᪥᪥᪥᪥᪥᪥᪥᪥᪥᪥᪥᪥᪥᪥᪥᪥᪥᪥᪥᪥᪥᪥᪥᪥

Nicely-Nicely

ALL OF us have our blind spots which cost us much in pleasure. Among mine, as *Guys and Dolls* * has persuaded me, is the fact that I never happen to have been a Damon Runyon man. This used to condemn me to a certain loneliness, since most of my friends were his admirers. Admirers? That is a niggardly understatement. These Runyon fans were devotees and idolators of the master. Their knowledge of the alphabet was not greater than their familiarity with the Broadway and sporting-life figures who color his stories.

My friends could spout Runyon as if they were old Shakespearean actors quoting the Bard. Their faces were all smiles when they did so or when they talked their own version of that special language which is Runyonese. I used to listen to them with amazement. Had they been exchanging jokes in

* *Guys and Dolls*, a musical fable of Broadway, based on a story and characters by Damon Runyon. Staged by George S. Kaufman. Music and lyrics by Frank Loesser. Book by Jo Swerling and Abe Burrows. Dances and musical numbers staged by Michael Kidd. Settings and lighting by Jo Mielziner. Costumes by Alvin Colt. Presented by Feuer and Martin. With a cast including Robert Alda, Vivian Blaine, Sam Levene, Isabel Bigley, Pat Rooney, Sr., B. S. Pully, Stubby Kaye, Tom Pedi, Johnny Silver, Paul Reed, Netta Packer, etc. At the Forty-Sixth Street Theatre, New York City. Opened November 24, 1950.

Polish, I could not have been more left out. Much as I tried to, I was unable to see what they saw in Runyon. I could muster no interest in his people and no enthusiasm for his style. I suffered by being excluded, as minorities will.

Guys and Dolls has convinced me that I must have been wrong. It may not as yet have made a Runyon convert of me, but most definitely it has turned me into a *Guys and Dolls* man. With complete enthusiasm I find myself on the side of its angels, its creators, its performers, and everyone who has had anything to do with it. And why not? No musical comedy I remember has been easier to relish than this "fable of Broadway" which has its origins in Damon Runyon.

How faithful its book is to the stories collected and published under this same title, I have no way of knowing because of that old distaste of mine (as irrational as any other allergy) which these many years has denied me the delights of feeding on Runyon. But I do know that I have seldom seen a musical which I enjoyed more or which on every count succeeded in doing more completely exactly what it set out to do.

As revealed in *Guys and Dolls,* Damon Runyon's is a special world within a special world. It is a segment of a segment which stretches from Forty-Second Street to Columbus Circle. It is a realm where men are guys, women are dolls, and gambling—big-time or small-scale—is a profession taken as much for granted as medicine or the law. Its people are the brassiest of city slickers. Inasmuch as they are as loud-mouthed as they are loudly dressed, they seem tough.

Doubtless they would be as tough as they seem, were it not for the curious innocence they retain. Questionable as their employment and their morals may be from a Sunday-school point of view, their basic goodness is beyond question. They are the most naive of underworldlings. In fact, they are touts and tinhorns who, however appalling, are so appealing that it seems safe to say even Mayor LaGuardia would have smiled upon them. Their heart-of-gold goodness may subtract from their reality, but it adds to the amusements they provide because it makes acceptance of them effortless.

The evening's faintly fairy-tale quality is enhanced by the over-fancy words these mugs speak in sentences which retreat without warning from elegance and grammar. This fairy-tale quality is further strengthened by the tandem romances out of which Jo Swerling and Abe Burrows have fabricated a plot. The first of these tells how a gambler at last finds time to marry a night club entertainer to whom he has been engaged for fourteen years. The second, the more lyric of the two, chronicles the courtship of another gambler who, to his surprise and the disbelief of his crap-shooting cronies, loses his heart to a beautiful lassie who labors in a mission.

There is a kind of music to the very names of the males in *Guys and Dolls*. Take, for example, Nicely-Nicely Johnson, Rusty Charlie, Harry the Horse, Nathan Detroit, or Angie the Ox. More than being a moniker, each of these is a jukebox melody. Equally fabulous are the clothes worn by these dice-artists. They are such suits as Broadway itself has never seen except in nightmares. Their colors are violent, their stripes wide as bridle paths, their vests cut as low as evening gowns.

All musical comedies present reviewers and their readers with ugly problems. But the gayer the musical, the more it seems fated to suffer in print. The reasons for this are obvious enough. Productions which are meant only as time-passers, "shows" whose justification is that they are "shows," are reduced to words. Before they are written these words are condemned to dullness because they attempt the impossible. They seek to analyze or describe in separate and static terms those fast-moving and fused pleasures which were designed to win laughter, to fill the eyes, and to enchant the ears.

Unification of the services, which is our military aim, is a theatrical fact in a production such as *Guys and Dolls*. This is made jubilantly and excitingly clear in and at every turn throughout the evening. Yet, when it comes to untangling these intertwined sources of enjoyment in the hope of giving credit where credit is due, the resulting inventory is bound to make as dry reading as a laundry list.

Even so, gratitude and admiration force me to run the risk. I cannot praise too highly the ease, flow, and sparkle of Jo Swerling's and Abe Burrows's book; the dash and gaiety of Frank Loesser's lyrics and music, especially in so hilarious a number as "Take Back Your Mink" ("to from whence it came"); the style and energy of Michael Kidd's dance numbers, with particular approval for his distinguished staging of the crap game ballet which lends a hitherto unsuspected glamour to its sewer background; the imagination and color of the settings and costumes of Jo Mielziner and Alvin Colt; and the wonderful skill and precision with which George S. Kaufman has directed the whole proceedings.

My enthusiasm for *Guys and Dolls* is such that I must toss bouquets in an equally wholesale manner at the large cast which the producers could not possibly improve upon if they sat up nights trying to do so. Although to particularize is unfair, some mention must be made of so delightful a newcomer as Isabel Bigley, who is enchanting as the lassie with the tambourine; of Vivian Blaine, whose night club entertainer is as superior a doll as can be found; and of Robert Alda and the ever dependable Sam Levene, both of whom play their gamblers with a gloriously funny mixture of that toughness and sweetness which makes the whole mood and approach of *Guys and Dolls* so different from the unflagging cynicism of *Pal Joey*. Just where the secondary touts and tinhorns were recruited, I cannot guess, but certainly the place of their unearthing was the right one.

It would be easy and it is tempting to raise the ante in a discussion of *Guys and Dolls* and to speak of it in long-haired terms as an example of popular art. But I happen to like it far too much to spoil anyone's fun, including my own, by doing so. Let me content myself with saying simply—it is not only grand entertainment, it is grand.

December 23, 1950

HOW TO BREAK with convention and get along quite nicely, thank you, without a hero and a heroine, or any surrenders to sentimentality.

In a Class by Itself

"THE catastrophe is manifestly wrong, for an Opera must end happily," says the Player who at the end of *The Beggar's Opera* is horrified to learn that Macheath, the polygamist, highwayman, scoundrel, and jailbreaker, is to be hanged.

"Your objection is very just," replies the Beggar, thereupon arranging, however absurdly, a reprieve and having the prisoner brought back in triumph to the several women who think they are married to him. "All this we must do," adds the Player, "to comply with the Taste of the Town."

The taste of the town, whether in the London of John Gay's time or the New York of John O'Hara's, has almost always been in the realm of musicals for spangled nonsense, for plots with happy endings and no relation to life, and for sweet romances about young men and maidens who, however nitwitted, are passed off because of their virtue as heroes and heroines. This is why Mr. O'Hara must be welcomed with Mr. Gay as an innovator.

Did Mr. Gay ignore prettiness and choose a Hogarthian world of squalor for his scene? Did he stand the operatic convention of his day on its flat head by dealing lustily and uproariously with bandits, jailbirds, pickpockets, sluts, and rogues? He did, and with a result which, more than making Gay rich and Rich (his producer) gay according to the contemporary gag, has been cherished as a classic all these many years.

The musical play * which Mr. O'Hara fashioned eleven years ago from his *New Yorker* sketches, and for which Richard Rodgers wrote some of his most beguiling music and the late Lorenz Hart some of his most engaging lyrics, has already been accepted as a modern classic. Certainly his *Pal Joey* is the nearest Broadway has come to producing its own *Beggar's Opera*. No less certainly, one of the surest sources of its enchantment is the utterly disenchanted evening it provides.

The night club entertainer who is its central figure has no more relation to morality than Lady Godiva, at least on the occasion of a not forgotten ride, had to clothing. He is a cad, a heel, a braggart, a liar, a rabbit, and a gigolo. The world through which he moves is the world of hotspots in Chicago. With the exception of one nice girl who has the sense to turn him down, the people he knows are a shady lot. They include striptease molls, blackmailers, drunks, and a rich society matron whose habit is to forget that she is married and whose kindnesses to young men exceed the call of charity.

Mr. O'Hara observes these people and their underworld with brilliant and hilarious remorselessness. He writes about them with such commendable detachment and honesty that his book could probably stand on its own as a play without the aid

* *Pal Joey*, a revival of the musical play. Music by Richard Rodgers. Lyrics by Lorenz Hart. Book by John O'Hara. Dances and musical numbers staged by Robert Alton. Settings by Oliver Smith. Costumes by Miles White. Book directed by David Alexander. Entire production supervised by Mr. Alton. Presented by Jule Styne and Leonard Key in association with Anthony B. Farrell. With a cast including Vivienne Segal, Harold Lang, Lionel Stander, Helen Gallagher, Pat Northrop, Elaine Stritch, Helen Wood, Jack Waldron, etc. At the Broadhurst Theatre, New York City. Opened January 3, 1952.

of music. To make such an experiment would, however, be a pity. It would mean losing such delightful Rodgers and Hart songs as "I Could Write a Book," "You Mustn't Kick It Around," "Chicago," "In Our Little Den," "Take Him," and of course "Bewitched, Bothered and Bewildered." No one in his right senses would want to be deprived of such numbers as these. Or, for that matter, of the bursting vitality, the brassiness, and the humor of the dancing as directed by Robert Alton.

Not all of us were bright enough to recognize the full merits of *Pal Joey* when it was first produced. I know I didn't, in spite of Richard Watts's valiant effort to make me see the light. It wasn't that I was shocked; it was merely that I was dumb. With bowed head and blushing face I have just reread the first-night review I wrote for the *New York Post*. I gather from that sorry notice that, though I enjoyed the first half, *Pal Joey* died for me thereafter. How completely I had missed the musical's point may be guessed from a line which complained that as the evening progressed Joey ceased to be a pal. What such a statement meant I have fortunately forgotten. One thing is certain. It was and is nonsense. Pal Joey was never meant to be the pal of anyone on either side of the footlights. Mr. O'Hara's title is a storm warning of ironies to come.

Before the initial production had run its course I did begin to realize I was wrong. How wrong, the current revival has made even clearer to me. For *Pal Joey* is far more than an enjoyable show. It is a distinguished contribution. It is distinguished in its music, its lyrics, its choreography, its writing, and once again in the manner in which it is acted, sung, and danced.

Vivienne Segal, as the Chicago matron, is if anything slimmer, trimmer, and more attractive than she was eleven years ago. Never dodging the sordid truths of the part, she projects them with a fine unfrightened gusto and yet maintains an assurance so quiet and well controlled that it has a dignity of its own. Right throughout the evening to the point of being irreplaceable, her singing of "Bewitched, Bothered and Bewildered" is a notable experience.

Harold Lang may fail to bring to the young night club entertainer the dark driving power that Gene Kelly had. Even so, his Pal Joey has its own excellence. He is as conscienceless as he should be, a figure with the right, cheap charm and easy smile who is spiritually shoddy. No one who saw him in *Look, Ma, I'm Dancin'* can be surprised at his incredible skill as a dancer. Let the music begin and his response to it is immediate and complete. His energy is matched only by his grace. The law of gravity is one of the many laws his Pal Joey disregards.

It may seem unfair to set this Rodgers-Hart-O'Hara work on a pedestal apart, when so admirable an underworld musical as *Guys and Dolls* is one of the current theatre's most popular and prized productions. But, without meaning to subtract in any way from the joys and merits of the latter, it must be confessed that there is a difference. Grandly tough and superbly gaudy as they are, the touts and tinhorns in *Guys and Dolls* have hearts as large as valentines. They are sentimentalists who just happen to be mugs.

No such inner core of tenderness is present in *Pal Joey*. Equally delightful though it is, it is pitched in quite another key. The toughness of its characters is more than skin deep. Their minds are tough, their speech is tough, their hearts are hard, and their lives as calloused as their points of view. A major contributor to the evening's fun is the utter and undeviating honesty with which Mr. O'Hara has dared to record the sordid world and nature of his night club entertainer. So unflinching is Mr. O'Hara, and hence so right, that *Pal Joey* has had no imitators. When it comes to predecessors, one must, as already pointed out, go back over all those years to John Gay's *The Beggar's Opera,* which was also diamond-hard and diamond-bright.

February 2, 1952

The Pen and the Sword

THE CONFUSIONS of being both at peace and at war, and the new demands made upon us by the uncertainties of the present.

꙳꙳꙳꙳꙳꙳꙳꙳꙳꙳꙳꙳꙳꙳꙳꙳꙳꙳꙳꙳꙳꙳꙳꙳꙳꙳꙳꙳꙳꙳꙳꙳꙳

The Two Fronts

THE SKY is cloudless here today. Everything in this little New England village seems as enduringly serene as the white houses, chaste and charming, on Main Street or as the tranquil elms which have long shaded them. The lawns are a soothing green, the fences gaily festooned with ramblers. Sailboats are scurrying across the blinding blue of the harbor. The tennis courts at the club are all taken, the pier is dotted with bathers. The sidewalks are brightened by people who have replaced their somber city clothes with those more colorful indulgences which the country and the seashore invite. Man and Nature, it would appear, are on vacation, relishing the summer's ease, relaxing from the winter's rigors.

But the sense of worries laid aside and peace complete is only an illusion. No sky is cloudless now. The storm, however distant by the map, is present in everyone's mind and heart. Its thunder is a part of every conversation. Only the littlest children do not hear it. On the beaches (their kind of beaches) they still pile up their edifices of sand, expecting them to withstand the encroachments of the next wave. The rest of us see the darkness in the sunshine's midst. The calm around us cannot shield us from the gale. We know, even when we are on vacation, that no one anywhere can at present take a vacation from the world.

We live, as we have grown accustomed to living, strangely double lives. Most of us as yet continue to live the personal and professional lives we cherish by the standards and with the interests, the hopes, the pleasures, the friendships, and the family affections made possible by the semblance of peace. But we also live that other life, the life which the headlines proclaim and the combat stories tell. We live engulfed in the repeated pattern, sickened by its having to repeat itself within less than a short five years. We live once more waiting for communiqués, scanning maps blackened by battle lines, and drawn by apprehension to our radios.

We live conscious of the young dying again, of courage tested daily, of homes disrupted, of troops moving, of greater armies forming, of civilians ceasing to be civilians in order to form them, and of plans being drawn up for the defense or evacuation of our cities. We live with talk of controls, priorities, and rationing, and with the contemptible selfishness of hoarders having already reappeared.

We live, if we are young men, under the threat of having our education, our professions, and our dreams suspended. If we are older and have seen it once or twice, we live, however great our melancholy, feeling deep within ourselves the insistent restlessness of the desire to be part of it, if it must be, yet dreading to be told that we are too old. Such news is in itself a kind of death. We live close to the conflict though an ocean and a continent away from it, aware of what is happening there and what may well happen elsewhere—and here. We live with the recognition of the future's uncertainty, certain only of our beliefs and that all we believe in may again be imperiled.

Living this dual life is not easy for anyone. No wonder parents, if they have sons, find themselves looking at them with a terrible intentness. Or that these sons, if they are in college or about to go there, discover that it is impossible to give their whole minds to their studies. No wonder their older brothers, starting out on their first jobs or at last in the swing of the jobs to which they returned when they got out of uniform, cannot apply themselves as wholeheartedly as once they might. No wonder, for that matter, that their fathers and mothers and all people worthy of being described as citizens scrutinize their own employment and question values which in ordinary peacetime they would accept.

To be at war openly and to the full is one thing; to be at peace, real peace, another. To be at both is disquieting (to put it mildly) if for no other reason than that it is confusing. Those working in industries held to be essential or capable of quick conversion to war effort are spared these confusions. As vital participants, they can hold their heads high. They enjoy the pride which comes from making a definite contribution. They can count themselves among the indispensables. Accordingly, they are not torn with doubts and are free from that sense of futility and irrelevance to which so many of us are heir as we face our everyday duties.

Values can be altered by environment no less than circumstance. Brooks Atkinson, a wise man blessed with a rare spirit, long ago realized this and stated it admirably in his book, *The Cingalese Prince*. In 1933 Mr. Atkinson escaped from the confinements of the island of Manhattan. As an active philosopher and vacationing critic, he circumnavigated the globe on a British freighter, the name of which he gave to his record of the voyage.

The Pen and the Sword

Plowing across the Pacific at the thirty-sixth parallel (not the thirty-eighth), Mr. Atkinson considered, among other things, the strange changes which can overtake literature in the presence of nature's immensity when men and their works are rudely reduced in scale. "Literature," he concluded, "is a bloodless subterfuge when you are plunged into the sources from which literature derives. . . . The treasures of literature need protection from the sun. Like leaves detached from a tree, the leaves of a book curl at the edges and grow sere when the sun beats directly on them. . . . Literature is put to the test every time a man puts out to sea."

If Mr. Atkinson found that light reading was not heavy enough for him on a ship of the *Cingalese Prince's* tonnage; if he discovered that he could not hear clever books above the wind roaring against his porthole; if the steady pulse of the engine compelled him to distrust sentences which were too self-conscious, and the language he came to like was made up of plain, simple, and straightforward words, we just now are in a position to understand those shifts in emphasis a new environment forced upon him. We are deeply conscious of them ourselves, brought about as they have been by recent events, current happenings, and the awareness of future possibilities. We, too, are somewhat at sea. We, too, can hear the roar of engines frightening in their might. We, too, face a typhoon that may be too large even for the Pacific to hold.

If, as Mr. Atkinson says, literature is put to the test every time a man puts out to sea, literature and all the arts and the values of civilized living are put to the test every time a nation faces the threats of war. Assuredly, we all know that we live in times when actions count most and many absorptions and professions seem extraneous. They are pushed to the periphery by crisis, and rightly so. If a robber breaks into our homes or if our houses are on fire, we would be worse than fools to continue reading a book (any book), listening to a symphony (any symphony), or admiring the colors and composition of a painting (any painting). Just now our very survival as a nation may be at stake. This is a chilling fact which all of us must accept. We have no other choice than to ready ourselves for whatever the future may hold.

But our sense of danger, proper though it is, can itself tempt us dangerously. However natural the initial impulses may be at moments of national crisis to question all the refinements of peacetime existence; however inevitable is the instinct to jettison what is loosely identified as "culture" when confronted anew with the barbarisms of conflict; however human are the reflexes which challenge the right of beauty, learning, and enlightenment to exist side by side with the brutal ugliness of battle, the first and perhaps final surrender any of us can make would be to lose sight, in the midst of war or the fears of war, of the true values of peace.

Win we must, and at whatever cost and however the conflict may be fought. Yet in the course of winning we must take special pains not to confuse the fight itself with the reasons for our fighting. This would be to rob our ultimate victory of its point and justification. We may not read at present or in the months ahead the same books which might have held our attention. Indeed, many may find they have scant time for reading at all. But not only books which speak to us about our troubled days but books from other ages which remind us of what is enduring in man, of his potentialities and dignity as an individual, and of what is mightiest, best, or most human in his thinking, his aspirations, his sufferings, or his behavior seem to me to gain importance rather than to lose it at present. So do all the arts. So do all the pursuits and occupations which are proofs that man lives by other laws and other impulses than those of the jungle.

Every modern war, however fortunate its outcome for us, has changed the world by subtracting from it abidingly. Every modern war has had to represent, in order to be won, a temporary abdication of ethical and humane standards. Every modern war has, in other words, demanded a certain retreat even of its victors and meant that they have lost in the very process of winning. Each modern war (certainly the next one will do so when and if it comes) has brought us nearer and nearer, in spite of all the progress man has made, to a new dark age. As Irwin Edman, a fine teacher, philosopher, and friend, recently wrote me, "It has suddenly dawned on me that since my sophomore year in college peace has come to seem abnormal in the world. Young men in their twenties must regard it as remote and as purely historical as we in our time regarded war."

We must not, we cannot, forget that regardless of the black storm clouds the lamps still burn and brightly burn. One of our major duties, along with all the other arduous ones which may lie ahead, is to shield these lamps from the gale.

Events, our own consciences, or those in authority will tell us if the time comes what each and all of us may have to do. Meanwhile the teacher must teach twice as hard and twice as persuasively as he has in the past. The student, still free to learn about other than military subjects, must study twice as diligently. Writers must write, painters must paint, musicians play, and architects build better than they have. All of us must mobilize ourselves to go about our tasks while they remain peaceful, hoping that in some small way we may contribute to the holding of those other lines, which are not the battle lines but the reason for forming battle lines.

August 12, 1950

Index

Index

Billy Budd, 186-192
Billy Budd, Foretopman, 189, 191
Bing, Rudolf, 129-130
Black-and-White, 14
Blaine, Vivian, 231
Blitzstein, Marc, 101
Body Snatchers, The, 28, 30
Bolm, Adolph, 54
Bosan, Alonzo, 197
Boston Transcript, 38
Boswell, James, 68
Boy David, The, 19
Boyer, Charles, 77, 84
Bradford, Roark, 193-195, 197
Broadway Scrapbook, 38
Brook, Lyndon, 94
Brown, Pamela, 113, 118, 119
Brownlee, John, 130
Brynner, Yul, 226
Buckmaster, John, 75
Burrows, Abe, 230, 231
Burton, Richard, 119
Byron, Lord, 8

C

Caesar, Julius, 63, 70
Caesar and Cleopatra, 68, 89-97
Calhern, Louis, 98-104
Camille, 182
Candida, 68
Capp, Al, 141, 157
Carlyle, Thomas, 8, 133
Carmen, 130
Carousel, 221
Cecil, Lord David, 8
Century Theatre, 123
Chapman, Robert, 191
Chapter on Dreams, A, 30

Charmides, 200
Cherry Orchard, The, 110
Child's Garden of Verses, A, 28, 34
Christmas Stories, 136
Chronicle of Friendships, A, 27
Churchill, Winston Spencer, 69
Cibber, Colley, 55
Cinderella, 154-157
Cingalese Prince, The, 38, 243-244
Clanton, Ralph, 94
Clark, Kendall, 75
Clash by Night, 168
Clermont, 42
Clouds, The, 201
Cochran, C. B., 54
Cocktail Party, The, 22, 108, 114
Coleridge, Samuel Taylor, 29
Collector's Progress, 3-10
Colt, Alvin, 231
Comic books, 141-151
Command Decision, 170
Conant, James Bryant, 153
Connelly, Marc, 193-198
Conroy, Frank, 216
Coppée, François, 38
Corneille, Pierre, 44
Cornell, Katharine, 76, 93-94
Cosi fan tutte, 127-131
Cosmic Yankee, 38
Country Girl, The, 167-171
Courage, 19
Coward, Noel, 226
Coxe, Louis O., 191
Crime and Punishment, 163
Critias, 200
Crito, 202
Croker, John Wilson, 8

Index

Fry, Christopher, 112-113, 117-119, 120-124
Furse, Roger, 89, 96, 123

G

Gabel, Martin, 101
Garrick, David, 113
Gay, John, 233, 237
Gémier, Firmin, 180
George, Henry, 51, 52, 63
George Selwyn and His Contemporaries, 8
Gerard, Rolf, 130
Gide, André, 172
Gielgud, John, 101, 113, 118, 119
Gladstone, William E., 28
Glass Menagerie, The, 161
Glyn, Elinor, 54
God That Failed, The, 172-173
Goethe, Johann Wolfgang von, 162
Golden Boy, 168
Goldoni's *Memoirs*, 55
Gondoliers, The, 162
Gone with the Wind, 93
Gorky, Maxim, 179
Gozzi's *Memoirs*, 55
Graham, Martha, 54, 56
Green Bay Tree, The, 93
Green Pastures, The, 193-198
Griffin, John W., 145-147, 150
Grock, 66
Guarrera, Frank, 130
Gulliver's Travels, 143
Guys and Dolls, 228-232

H

Hagen, Uta, 76, 170
Hamilton, Clayton, 19

Hamlet, 71, 75, 93, 108-109
Hammerstein, Oscar, 2nd, 54, 221-227
Hammond, Percy, 223
Hardwicke, Sir Cedric, 77, 84, 93, 95
Harris, Frank, 72
Harris, Julie, 207-212
Harrison, Rex, 123
Harrison, Richard B., 196
Hart, Lorenz, 234-236
Harvard Dramatic Club, 38
Harvard University, 107, 153
Hawkins, Jack, 107
Hazlitt, William, 69
Heartbreak House, 72
Hedda Gabler, 102, 110
Helpmann, Robert, 94, 96
Hemingway, Ernest, 44
Henley, W. E., 30, 34, 213
Henry Thoreau, 38
Henry V, 93
Henry VIII, 202
Heritage Press, 26
Hill, Steven, 171
Hitler, Adolf, 63
Homer, 64
Hope, Anthony, 15
Horst, Louis, 54
Houghton, Norris, 192
Houseman, John, 101
Howard, Sidney, 170
Huckleberry Finn, The Adventures of, 143, 147

I

I Am a Camera, 207-212
Ibsen, Henrik, 65, 154, 162, 199
Ideal Husband, An, 15

Index

Index

Index